Kipling and the Critics

Kipling

AND THE CRITICS

Edited and with an Introduction by

ELLIOT L. GILBERT

PETER OWEN—LONDON

PETER OWEN LTD   12 KENDRICK MEWS   KENDRICK PLACE
LONDON S.W. 7

I

It would be difficult to think of another artist, dead thirty years, who continues to be at once so popular and so cordially hated as Rudyard Kipling is today. Indeed, a compiler of literary reputation studies could not choose a more perplexing subject. Reputation studies usually follow certain familiar patterns. A writer, having failed to make his mark in his own lifetime, is posthumously raised to eminence by enlightened readers of a new generation. Or, alternatively, a writer, lionized for a few years by the fashionable world, slips irrecoverably into oblivion the moment the fashions change. Or, again, a writer, very popular in his own day, is temporarily eclipsed by younger artists, only to be returned at some later date, more secure than ever, to the company of the immortals. Many variations are possible on these basic patterns, but all stories of this sort seem inevitably to make the same point: that in the last analysis, it is not upon the adulation of the crowd but rather on the long-term respect of serious readers and responsible critics that literary survival depends.

Rudyard Kipling seems somehow to have circumvented this rule. Born one hundred years ago and already world-famous a mere twenty-five years later, he remains today—especially in Great Britain and (curiously) in the Soviet Union, but throughout the world as well—an extremely popular writer.[1] And this,

1 Indeed, no major work of his has ever been out of print—a remarkable record. For a comment on the Russian vogue for Kipling see R[oger] L[ancelyn] G[reen], "Kipling in Russia," *The Kipling Journal*, xxix, No. 143 (September 1962), 4.

despite the fact that the political views with which his name is commonly associated are considered old-fashioned, if not actually dangerous, by many readers, and despite the fact, too, that though he and his works have been the subject of important essays by such formidable critics as Henry James, T. S. Eliot, Edmund Wilson, Bonamy Dobrée, C. S. Lewis, Lionel Trilling, and most recently J. I. M. Stewart, he has never enjoyed, and does not enjoy today—except among a very few—any serious critical reputation.

That a definitive appraisal and judgment of Kipling the artist has so long been delayed—the writer died in 1936 but most readers assume the event took place several decades earlier— can in part be explained by the fact that both the author and his books are almost always dealt with in a political context, and politics notoriously has a way of making it difficult to arrive at sober judgments. One effect of the obscurity which so often descends upon a writer soon after his death is to permit the strong but ephemeral passions which surrounded him during his lifetime to spend themselves; thus the critics of a new generation are freed for the job of viewing the man and his work with detachment. Kipling has never had such a cooling-off period. Though many of the political views which he held (or is presumed on the evidence of his poems and stories to have held) seem to us to be as much a part of the dead past as the events which inspired them, the great issues of self-government, of "emerging populations," and so on, to which these views constitute one response, are still very much alive. As a result Kipling seems, even to those people who consider his ideas reprehensibly out-of-date, a strangely contemporary writer, a contributor, so to speak, to the current debate, whose views must urgently be opposed. Under these circumstances, calm appraisal of him becomes almost impossible, and the question of his reputation continues to be caught up in the same passions which marked criticism of his work almost from the first.

II

To be sure, some of the very earliest criticism was fairly objective. It took a while for Kipling to develop into a *bête noire*, and so few of the first commentaries were temperately critical rather than destructive, judiciously enthusiastic rather than fanatic. Andrew Lang's brief essay "Mr. Kipling's Stories," for example, still holds up rather well, striking the modern reader, who has much more of Kipling's work to go on than Lang had, as a quite reasonable statement about the new author and his art. Lang seems to have made a specialty of directing attention to Kipling. He conducted a monthly column for *Longman's Magazine* called "At the Sign of the Ship," in which in October, 1886, he referred favorably to an exciting new collection of poems recently arrived from India and printed anonymously under the title *Departmental Ditties*. It is likely that this was the first critical notice to be taken of Kipling anywhere in England. Later, on March 25th, 1890, the *London Times* published an unsigned and nearly unprecedented leading article welcoming a brilliant young Anglo-Indian writer to the world of literature and commenting on the whole range of his work. One scholar, an authority on both men, thinks it probable that the author of this influential and eminently temperate piece on Kipling was Lang.

Another early critic whose attitude combined controlled enthusiasm with watchful waiting was Henry James. James was a personal friend of Kipling's; he was, in fact, best man at Kipling's wedding. And so when the younger author's problems with pirated American editions of his works made it necessary for him in 1891 to bring out a volume of his short stories in New York, James was persuaded to contribute a critical introduction to the book. The job was a delicate one. The novelist genuinely admired his young protégé, writing of him to his brother William as "the most complete man of genius" he had ever known. But he was also troubled about the direction which Kipling's genius seemed to be taking, and it is amusing to see, in this Introduction, James' famous involuted style for once being used deliberately to conceal rather than to illuminate—to conceal the fact, elsewhere expressed with vigor and frankness,[2] of his misgivings about his subject's future.

2 On Kipling's appearance in London in 1890, James wrote a letter to Samoa announcing that the new Stevenson had arrived and urging the old one to return home. Somewhat later, he sent a second letter advising

Of course no trace of these doubts appears in his friendly essay, unless what James omits to say may be construed as adverse criticism. He makes, with charm, at great length, and using many elaborate figures of speech, a number of insightful remarks about Kipling, about his youth and the novelty of his subject matter, and about the brilliance of such a portrait as Mulvaney's. Only at the moment when he must offer some general appraisal of the young author does he literally vanish in a tremendous burst of camouflaging verbiage, to advance upon us again the next instant, smiling affably, from a wholly new direction. Confronted, for example, with the need to say something about Kipling's prospects, he is able to produce the remarkable statement that

There is nothing in the world (for the prophet) so charming as to prophesy, and as there is nothing so inconclusive, the tendency should be repressed in proportion as the opportunity is good. There is a certain want of courtesy to a peculiarly contemporaneous present even in speculating, with a dozen deferential precautions, on the question of what will become in the later hours of the day of a talent that has got up so early.

The passage goes on to develop the metaphor of early rising, and the reader may easily finish the essay without realizing that James has skillfully refused to commit himself.

III

The essays by Lang and James, however, are not typical of early criticism of Kipling, criticism which fell, for the most part, into one of two categories: bitter attacks on the young author for his political and social attitudes, and enthusiastic, sometimes triumphantly know-nothing defenses of these same attitudes. Perhaps the best example of the split personality and the political orientation of this early criticism is the angry exchange of views between Robert Buchanan and Sir Walter Besant, collected under the title *The Voice of "The Hooligan."* Buchanan was a Scottish author-critic, some twenty-five years

---

R. L. S. that he might stay where he was. See *The Letters of Henry James,* ed. Percy Lubbock (New York, 1920), pp. 1, 156, 178, 188–189, 249, 270–271, 339, 341.

Kipling's senior, who, prior to his attack on the young man, had already achieved some success with poetry of his own, as well as a good deal of notoriety with what was considered a cruel assault on Dante Gabriel Rossetti's 1870 collection of poems. Apparently Kipling had enraged Buchanan as much as Rossetti had, though obviously for different reasons, and in 1900 there appeared over Buchanan's signature the caustic essay which he called "The Voice of the Hooligan."

The title represents Buchanan's thesis pretty fairly. In the writer's angry prose, Kipling is pictured as riding the crest of "a great back-wave" which is irresistibly sweeping civilization "in the direction of absolute barbarism." Further, the young author is characterized as one who, with his brutish jingoism and his cockney vulgarity, "adumbrates in his single person . . . all that is most deplorable, all that is most retrograde and savage, in the restless and uninstructed Hooliganism of the time."

Angry and often distorted as Buchanan's view of Kipling is, Sir Walter Besant's defense of his sometime protégé is in places even more intemperate. Besant was an important member of the literary establishment of his day—"a Dogberry of the Literary Watch" was Buchanan's less complimentary way of putting it—and his peremptory dismissal of his opponent conveys that very air of brutal insensitivity which Buchanan deplores in Kipling. Equally brutal is his defense of the young writer against the accusation of jingoism. In response to such an accusation, Besant might well have insisted upon literary rather than political standards of judgment, or, failing that, might have pointed out, as George Orwell was to do years later, that the accuracy and realism of Kipling's portrayal of men under fire—of their agony and terror—were enough to dispel any reader's romantic notions about war. Instead, he makes the remarkable statement that "a time may come when war will not be a necessity—but that time is not yet. . . . There are worse evils than war. . . . The poisonous weeds that grow rank in times of peace corrupt the national blood," and so on. Thus did he see fit to defend Kipling against Buchanan's charge of Hooliganism.

Despite Besant's efforts, however, Buchanan's approach to Kipling proved influential. Beginning as it did with an assump-

tion that the young author was "on the side of all that is
ignorant, selfish, base and brutal in the instincts of humanity,"
and then hunting up evidence, often in the form of quotations
taken out of context, to justify what was, in the first place, an
extraliterary judgment, it conceived of the writer less as a man
of letters than as a person with great political, social, and moral
influence who also happens to write, and as such it became a
model—a grotesque model, to be sure—for much later criticism.
Boris Ford's often incisive essay in *Scrutiny*, for example, seems
to be partly in this tradition, with its wartime proposal (omitted
in the present revision), that Kipling's works be banned for the
duration. And H. E. Bates' effort, in his book *The Modern
Short Story*, to equate Kipling with Adolph Hitler because the
two men had an interest in swastikas, is plainly in the spirit of
"The Voice of the Hooligan."

Moreover, because of his association with political ideas,
Kipling suffered, as he continues to suffer, more than most
writers, from what Henry James once called "the stupid superstition that the amiability of a story-teller is the amiability of
the people he represents—that their vulgarity, or depravity, or
fatuity, or gentility are tantamount to the same qualities in the
story-teller himself." Critics have long equated certain brutal
or violent attitudes on the part of characters in Kipling's works
with the author's own attitudes. Some, like Buchanan, have
gone so far as to extract from these attitudes a political credo,
which they have then offered as the author's own. Especially
in the early days, this sort of error had constantly to be met
and put down. On one occasion, Oscar Wilde, having con-
gratulated Kipling on his delineation of Anglo-Indians, and
having remarked that "as one turns over the pages of . . .
Plain Tales from the Hills, one feels as if one were seated under
a palm tree, reading life by superb flashes of vulgarity," found
it necessary to explain, to an irate correspondent in the *Times*,
that by writing about vulgar Anglo-Indians neither he nor
Kipling meant to imply that every Englishman in India was
vulgar.

Besant's defense of Kipling also influenced later critics, as it
was itself influenced by an early and well-established tradition
of immoderate praise of the young author, praise which seldom

got much more profound than William Ernest Henley dancing about on his wooden leg in his enthusiasm for "Danny Deever," or than Professor Masson, "the grave commentator on Milton," waving a newspaper containing the same poem before the eyes of his amazed students and shouting "Here's Literature! Here's Literature at last!" What C. E. Carrington, Kipling's official biographer, has called "the first analytical essay by a writer who knew Kipling's background, and knew India," is typically concerned far more with making imperialist propaganda than with discussing art.

Some day a writer will arise, perhaps this young poet is the destined man, who will make that nobler Anglo-Indian world known as it really is. It will then be seen by what a hard discipline of endurance our countrymen and countrywomen in India are trained to do England's greatest work on earth. . . .

The fact that the author of these remarks was Sir William Hunter, an important figure in the Viceregal Council of India, established still another tradition in Kipling criticism, the tradition that the job of commenting favorably on the author's work should for the most part devolve not upon literary men but rather upon politicians and retired army officers, preferably those with Indian connections. Of such commentators, Lieutenant-General Sir George MacMunn, K.C.B., K.C.S.I., and D.S.O. was undoubtedly the champion. In addition to many books about India and the east, he produced a volume called *Kipling's Women* and another with the promising title *Rudyard Kipling: Craftsman*. Unfortunately, the latter does not fulfill its promise. Indeed, it is little more than a series of plot summaries, and at that, the sort of plot summaries in which kindly curtains are always being drawn over scenes too moving or too terrible to describe.

IV

How did Kipling respond to all of this comment? He seldom addressed himself formally to his critics, friendly or unfriendly, though he sometimes made his reactions to them known in his letters and verse. His delight, for example, at the astonishing London success of his work in 1890 is evident in the cable he despatched to India inviting his parents to come and witness his triumph for themselves. Characteristically, he telegraphed only the cryptic phrase "Genesis, xlv, 9." At Lahore, however, the joyous message was understood without difficulty.

Haste ye, and go up to my father, and say unto him, Thus saith thy son Joseph [Kipling's full name was Joseph Rudyard Kipling], God hath made me lord of all Egypt: come down unto me; tarry not.

His reaction to unfavorable criticism could be just as expressive, if, on occasion, a good deal more direct. It is, for instance, plainly disgust with members of the "Art for Art's Sake" movement, and their easy dismissal of his writings as vulgar and unaesthetic, that inspired the well-known stanza of "In Partibus:"

> But I consort with long-haired things
>   In velvet collar-rolls,
> Who talk about the Aims of Art,
>   And "theories" and "goals,"
> And moo and coo with women-folk
>   About their blessed souls.

If the verse is rather tasteless and impatient (though not conspicuously more so than many of the opinions that provoked it), Kipling was after all a young man at the time of its composition and had yet to adopt the stoic rule of the professional writer never publicly to respond to criticism.

By the time Max Beerbohm's attacks began in 1901, with the cartoon "De Arte Poetica. J[ohn] B[ull] to R[udyard] K[ipling]," Kipling had acquired greater self-control. Beerbohm, usually the most delicate of critics, whose chief literary tool was a gently wielded, if often wicked, irony, became uncharacteristically angry when he so much as spoke or thought about Rudyard Kipling, a man with whom, according to S. N. Behrman, he early entered into the only virulent relationship of his life. "His publication increased," Beerbohm reminisced regretfully to Behrman about Kipling. "So did my derogation. He didn't stop. I *couldn't* stop. I meant to. I wanted to. But I couldn't." Over a period of thirty years Beerbohm produced at least nine savage caricatures of the writer, two critical articles, and the ferocious but brilliant parody reprinted here. And in the face of all these attacks Kipling remained silent. That he was hurt there can be no question. Beerbohm himself reports passing Kipling in a carriage one day and seeing him quickly avert his eyes. And when David Low, the great British caricaturist, applied for permission to sketch the author, his request was denied because, according to Low, Kipling was still smarting from a cartoon of Max's done twenty years before. Yet Kipling never published a word in response to Beerbohm's obsessive criticism, knowing, perhaps, that to these all-too-familiar attacks on him as a political or cultural phenomenon no reply was possible.

To a critic, on the other hand, willing to consider seriously questions of craftsmanship or matters of art, Kipling could be exuberantly responsive and even pathetically grateful. His most demanding instructor in the difficult art of putting the best possible words in the best possible order was always his father, and whenever anyone else approached Lockwood Kipling in intensity of commitment to the craft of writing, the younger Kipling gave him all his respect. In 1897, for example, the *Atlantic Monthly* broke a long silence by publishing an article on Kipling by Charles Eliot Norton. The article had high praise for the young writer but also shrewdly analyzed his faults and suggested methods for improvement. Kipling's letter to Norton is all the more remarkable for having been addressed to the critic by a man who, at the time he composed the reply, was easily the most famous literary figure in the world. "We are both of us [R. K. and his wife] awed," he wrote,

and if the truth be told a little scared at your article in the *Atlantic Monthly*. . . . True it is, most sadly true that I have not been true to my duties, but I did not know that I had been so untrue. . . . You are the only man except my father and Uncle Ned [Edward Burne-Jones] whose disapproval or advice slays me; and I will say just as one says to one's father when one is little, "I'll try to think and be better next time." But, even now, the notion that *you* should have reviewed me rather makes me gasp.

Still, the letter to Norton was a private communication. If Kipling anywhere addressed his critics, all of his critics, publicly, seriously, and out of a deep sense of injustice, he did so in a late poem he called "The Appeal."

If I have given you delight
　　By aught that I have done,
Let me lie quiet in that night
　　Which shall be yours anon:

And for the little, little span
　　The dead are borne in mind,
Seek not to question other than
　　The books I leave behind.

The poem is first of all an appeal for that freedom from inquiry into purely personal affairs which Kipling sought all his life, especially in his last years, and in the pursuit of which first his wife and later his daughter destroyed much of his private correspondence and many of his papers. But if these few lines can be said to make still another appeal, they may perhaps be seen as expressing Kipling's hope that in the long run the judgment of history upon him might be based not on ephemeral political associations but on art, not on the opinions of those who know him only as the author of a few catch phrases but on the careful conclusions of those who have read his works critically and with respect. Not that Kipling would necessarily have objected to all politically oriented commentaries. The essays by Lionel Trilling and George Orwell included here, for instance, and such later works as Noel Annan's "Kipling's Place in the History of Ideas," [3] and Deutsch and Wiener's "The Lonely Nationalism of Rudyard Kipling" [4] show that this critical vein can be worked with some success. But there can be no doubt either that Kipling would have been pleased at the fairly recent development of a third kind of criticism of his works, a criticism founded on serious study of the books he left behind and motivated by the critics' real desire to make those books their chief concern.

v

In 1929, Bonamy Dobrée published a brilliant essay on Kipling in *The Lamp and the Lute*. In it, he offered many provocative insights into his subject's obsessive, central themes (man's loneliness, for instance, and the redemptive nature of

---

3 *Victorian Studies*, III, iv (1960), 323–348.
4 *Yale Review*, LII (1963), 499–517.

pain), but his major innovation was to speak of Kipling as a serious artist. Other reputable critics have been willing to begin their comments with grudging praise of Kipling's obvious power, but almost always they have concluded that the man's sins outweigh the artist's virtues. Professor Dobrée was the first critic, with a significant body of work to deal with, to reverse this procedure, granting at the outset his subject's faults but insisting that in spite of them he remained a major artist. Admitting and deploring, for example, the presence of cruelty in Kipling's work, he nevertheless reiterates that the author's real significance "resides in the fact that, as M. Andre Maurois has said, 'he has a permanent, natural contact with the oldest and deepest layers of human consciousness.' " The importance of this critical reversal must not be underestimated. Kipling's reputation among serious readers has languished for as long as it has precisely because so few commentators have been willing to commit themselves to the author as wholeheartedly as Dobrée.

One such commitment which mildly astonished the literary world when it first appeared in 1941 was that by T. S. Eliot in his *Choice of Kipling's Verse*, a volume compiled in an effort to rehabilitate the older writer's reputation as a poet, and perhaps also to tap the patriotic market then opening up. The astonishment of the literary world resulted from the fact that Eliot and Kipling—the former well-known to be an incomprehensible, modern poet, the latter a too-comprehensible, old-fashioned one—made what at first seemed strange bedfellows. Soon, however, critics—among them Boris Ford—were pointing out that Eliot and Kipling really had a good deal in common (their conservatism, their reliance upon ritual, and so on), and indeed, as Eliot himself reveals in the 1958 address published here, Kipling had long been one of his preoccupations.[5]

Other writers have followed Dobrée and Eliot in producing general surveys of Kipling's art, notably C. S. Lewis ("I have never at any time been able to understand how a man of taste could doubt that Kipling is a very great artist."), and Randall

5 J. Donald Adams, in his *Copey of Harvard* (Boston, 1960), has preserved for us an undergraduate essay of Eliot's on Kipling. See pp. 158–164.

Jarrell, to mention only those represented in this collection. Still others have turned from survey to close readings of individual texts. It is curious that, with the revolution in critical techniques which has gone on during the last forty years, Kipling's work should only now be coming in for such detailed study. The explanation is, of course, that one does not subject to close critical scrutiny works which don't seem, on the basis of their reputations, to deserve such attention, and it is only during the last few years that Kipling has come to be discussed to any great extent as an artist. Significantly, the Kipling who emerges from these textual analyses is quite different from the Kipling of popular fancy. This Kipling is an artist of considerable stature, one who has much to communicate to the modern reader and who communicates it chiefly through the structures of his works and the ordering of his material. We have only to compare Steven Marcus' comments on *Stalky & Co.* with those of Buchanan, or to put J. M. S. Tompkin's perceptive explication of "Dayspring Mishandled" beside the many casual dismissals of Kipling as a facile journalist, to see the virtue of criticism that is firmly rooted in a text. Other writers have also begun to produce such detailed studies—Paul Fussell, Jr.,[6] for example, and most recently C. A. Bodelsen.[7] It would be safe to say, however, that their critical activity is not so much representative of the first seventy-five years of Kipling commentary as it is a promise for the next seventy-five, a promise of material for some future anthology.

VI

The table of contents for the present anthology was, to a certain extent, determined by technical considerations. One of the most famous of all essays about Kipling, for example, Edmund Wilson's "The Kipling that Nobody Read," [8] had to be omitted because of its great length, while T. S. Eliot's Introduction to *A Choice of Kipling's Verse* was withheld by its author, in part out of his feeling that the piece should probably

6 "Irony, Freemasonry, and Humane Ethics in Kipling's 'The Man Who Would Be King,' " *ELH*, xxv, No. 1 (1958), 216–233.
    7 *Aspects of Kipling's Art* (New York, 1964).
    8 *The Wound and the Bow* (New York, 1947), pp. 105–181.

be rewritten before being published again separately. Instead, we have Mr. Eliot's charming and informative 1958 address to the Kipling Society (of which he was a Vice-President), an address which is now being published in book form for the first time, and for the first time in any form in America.

Considerations of space also made it necessary to slight such partisan or continental criticism of Kipling as Richard Le Gallienne's somewhat out-dated though still forceful, turn-of-the-century attack, *Rudyard Kipling: A Criticism,* W. J. Peddicord's contemptuously titled and, like Buchanan's assault, violently critical *Rudyard Reviewed,* and a number of fine French essays and book-length studies, among them André Maurois' "Rudyard Kipling," from his *Prophets and Poets,* André Chevrillon's "The Poetry of Rudyard Kipling" from *Three Studies in English Literature,* and the recent, brilliant *La Poétique de Rudyard Kipling* by Francis Léaud.

Obviously, an anthology as selective as this one must give an incomplete picture of the history of Kipling studies.[9] Yet if it at least succeeds in being representative of the Kipling criticism that has been produced in English during the last seventy-five years, it may help to explain the ambivalent attitude toward the author and his work which makes it possible for the man to be at once so very popular and so heartily disliked. We have already noted that Kipling criticism comes down to us in three essentially parallel (and too often mutually exclusive) traditions, traditions represented by Buchanan's attack, Besant's defense, and Dobrée's analysis, and it is precisely the exclusiveness of these traditions which makes a consensus on Kipling so difficult to achieve. Most signs today point to a growing interest in Kipling as an artist and to a certain lessening of emphasis on Kipling as a political phenomenon. If this is so, then perhaps G. S. Fraser indicates the way of the future when he speaks of the writer as one

who must be rediscovered from time to time and who, when the quarrels in which he so furiously engaged himself are forgotten,

9 For a complete listing of works about Kipling see *Rudyard Kipling: An Annotated Bibliography of Writings About Him,* ed. Helmut E. Gerber and Edward Lauterbach, *EFT,* III (1960), iii, 1–74; iv, 75–148; v, 149–235. A supplement will be published in 1965.

will be remembered for a passionate exactness of language and for disturbing moments of deep vision that every now and again break, with the most startling effect, through the compact and jaunty surfaces of his verse and prose.[10]

New York   E. L. GILBERT
March, 1965

---

10 *The Modern Writer and His World* (New York, 1953), p. 66 (note).

ANDREW LANG, a late nineteenth-century man of letters and author of such works as *Myth, Ritual and Religion* and *The History of Scotland*, helped to introduce Kipling to London literary society.

OSCAR WILDE was a brilliant critic as well as a novelist, playwright, and poet. His *Picture of Dorian Gray* and Kipling's *The Light That Failed* were both published in *Lippincott's Monthly Magazine* in 1890.

HENRY JAMES, the American novelist, was an early admirer and friend of Kipling's. His growing disillusionment with the young writer is recorded in his letters.

ROBERT BUCHANAN, a Scottish poet and critic, published *London Poems* in 1866 and his famous attack on Rossetti, *The Fleshly School of Poetry*, in 1871.

MAX BEERBOHM, a long-time critic of Kipling, produced many scathing caricatures of his subject and the harsh review, "Kipling's Entire," collected in *Around Theatres* in 1924.

BONAMY DOBRÉE, editor of *The Oxford History of English Literature* series and author of *English Literature in the Early Eighteenth Century*, has written a number of studies of Kipling, including a 1951 pamphlet for the British Council and the National Book League.

BORIS FORD, critic, essayist, and teacher, is Dean of the School of Educational Studies at the University of Sussex. He is the author of *The Pelican Guide to English Literature*.

GEORGE ORWELL is best known as the author of *Animal Farm* and *1984*. His critical essays customarily examine the political implications of literary works.

LIONEL TRILLING teaches English at Columbia University. He has written a definitive study of Matthew Arnold's life and works, as well as many other critical books and essays.

C. S. LEWIS, author of *English Literature in the Sixteenth Century*, is perhaps equally famous for such fiction as *Out of the Silent Planet* and for his popular discourse on religion and morality, *The Screwtape Letters*.

T. S. ELIOT, until his death a Vice-President of the Kipling Society, recently reissued his *Choice of Kipling's Verse*. A new edition of his collected poems was published in 1963.

J. M. S. TOMPKINS has written *The Art of Rudyard Kipling*, an authoritative and far-ranging study published in 1959. She is also the author of *The Popular Novel in England, 1700–1800*.

RANDALL JARRELL, National Book Award winner and Consultant in Poetry at the Library of Congress from 1956 to 1958, has edited a number of collections of Kipling's short stories.

STEVEN MARCUS, a member of the English Department at Columbia University and an editor of *Partisan Review*, is the author of *Dickens: From Pickwick to Dombey*.

ELLIOT L. GILBERT, who teaches English at Brooklyn College, has published a number of essays about Kipling and is at present completing a full-length study of Kipling as a short story writer.

CONTENTS

Kipling and the Critics

Andrew Lang

Mr. Kipling's Stories *

THE WIND bloweth where it listeth. But the wind of literary inspiration has rarely shaken the bungalows of India, as, in the
tales of the old Jesuit missionaries, the magical air shook the
frail "medicine tents," where Huron conjurors practised their
mysteries. With a world of romance and of character at their
doors, Englishmen in India have seen as if they saw it not. They
have been busy in governing, in making war, making peace,
building bridges, laying down roads, and writing official reports.
Our literature from that continent of our conquest has been
sparse indeed, except in the way of biographies, of histories,
and of rather local and unintelligible *faceti*æ. Except the novels
by the author of "Tara," and Sir Henry Cunningham's brilliant
sketches, such as "Dustypore," and Sir Alfred Lyall's poems,
we might almost say that India has contributed nothing to our
finer literature. That old haunt of history, the wealth of character brought out in that confusion of races, of religions, and
the old and new, has been wealth untouched, a treasure-house
sealed: those pagoda trees have never been shaken. At last there
comes an Englishman with eyes, with a pen extraordinarily deft,
an observation marvellously rapid and keen; and, by good luck,
this Englishman has no official duties: he is neither a soldier, nor
a judge; he is merely a man of letters. He has leisure to look
around him, he has the power of making us see what he sees;
and, when we have lost India, when some new power is ruling

* [From *Essays in Little* (London, 1891), pp. 198–205.]

where we ruled, when our empire has followed that of the Moguls, future generations will learn from Mr. Kipling's works what India was under English sway.

It is one of the surprises of literature that these tiny master-pieces in prose and verse were poured, "as rich men give that care not for their gifts," into the columns of Anglo-Indian journals. There they were thought clever and ephemeral—part of the chatter of the week. The subjects, no doubt, seemed so familiar, that the strength of the handling, the brilliance of the colour, were scarcely recognised. But Mr. Kipling's volumes no sooner reached England than the people into whose hands they fell were certain that here were the beginnings of a new literary force. The books had the strangeness, the colour, the variety, the perfume of the East. Thus it is no wonder that Mr. Kipling's repute grew up as rapidly as the mysterious mango tree of the conjurors. There were critics, of course, ready to say that the thing was merely a trick, and had nothing of the supernatural. That opinion is not likely to hold its ground. Perhaps the most severe of the critics has been a young Scotch gentleman, writing French, and writing it wonderfully well, in a Parisian review. He chose to regard Mr. Kipling as little but an imitator of Bret Harte, deriving his popularity mainly from the novel and exotic character of his subjects. No doubt, if Mr. Kipling has a literary progenitor, it is Mr. Bret Harte. Among his earlier verses a few are what an imitator of the American might have written in India. But it is a wild judgment which traces Mr. Kipling's success to his use, for example, of Anglo-Indian phrases and scraps of native dialects. The presence of these elements is among the causes which have made Englishmen think Anglo-Indian literature tediously provincial, and India a bore. Mr. Kipling, on the other hand, makes us regard the continent which was a bore an enchanted land, full of marvels and magic which are real. There has, indeed, arisen a taste for exotic literature: people have become alive to the strangeness and fascination of the world beyond the bounds of Europe and the United States. But that is only because men of imagination and literary skill have been the new conquerors—the Corteses and Balboas of India, Africa, Australia, Japan, and the isles of the southern seas. All such conquerors, whether they write with the polish of M. Pierre Loti, or with the carelessness of Mr. Boldrewood, have, at least, seen new worlds for themselves; have gone out of the streets of the over-populated lands into the open air; have sailed and ridden, walked and hunted; have escaped from the fog and smoke of towns. New strength has come from fresher air into their brains and blood; hence the novelty and buoyancy of the stories which they tell. Hence, too, they are rather to be counted among romanticists than realists, however real is the essential truth of their books. They have found so much to see and to record, that they are not tempted to use the microscope, and pore for ever on the minute in character. A great deal of realism, especially in France, attracts because it is novel, because M. Zola and others have also found new worlds to conquer. But certain provinces in those worlds were not unknown to, but were voluntarily neglected by, earlier explorers. They were the "Bad Lands" of life and character: surely it is wiser to seek quite new realms than to build mud huts and dunghills on the "Bad Lands."

Mr. Kipling's work, like all good work, is both real and romantic. It is real because he sees and feels very swiftly and keenly; it is romantic, again, because he has a sharp eye for the reality of romance, for the attraction and possibility of adventure, and because he is young. If a reader wants to see petty characters displayed in all their meannesses, if this be realism, surely certain of Mr. Kipling's painted and frisky matrons are realistic enough. The seamy side of Anglo-Indian life: the intrigues, amorous or semi-political—the slang of the people who describe dining as "mangling garbage"—the "games of tennis with the seventh commandment"—he has not neglected any of these. Probably the sketches are true enough, and pity 'tis 'tis true: for example, the sketches in "Under the Deodars" and in "The Gadsbys." That worthy pair, with their friends, are to myself as unsympathetic, almost, as the characters in "La Conquête de Plassans." But Mr. Kipling is too much a true realist to make their selfishness and pettiness unbroken, unceasing. We know that "Gaddy" is a brave, modest, and hard-working soldier; and, when his little silly bride (who prefers being kissed by a man with waxed moustaches) lies near to death, certainly I am nearer to tears than when I

am obliged to attend the bed of Little Dombey or of Little
Nell. Probably there is a great deal of slangy and unrefined
Anglo-Indian society; and, no doubt, to sketch it in its true
colours is not beyond the province of art. At worst it is re-
deemed, in part, by its constancy in the presence of various
perils—from disease, and from "the bullet flying down the
pass." Mr. Kipling may not be, and very probably is not, a
reader of "Gyp"; but "The Gadsbys," especially, reads like the
work of an Anglo-Indian disciple, trammelled by certain English conventions. The more Pharisaic realists—those of the strictest sect—would probably welcome Mr. Kipling as a younger
brother, so far as "Under the Deodars" and "The Gadsbys"
are concerned, if he were not occasionally witty and even flippant, as well as realistic. But, very fortunately, he has not con-
fined his observation to the leisures and pleasures of Simla;
he has looked out also on war and on sport, on the life of all
native tribes and castes; and has even glanced across the borders
of "The Undiscovered Country."

Among Mr. Kipling's discoveries of new kinds of characters,
probably the most popular is his invention of the British soldier
in India. He avers that he "loves that very strong man, Thomas
Atkins"; but his affection has not blinded him to the faults of
the beloved. Mr. Atkins drinks too much, is too careless a
gallant in love, has been educated either too much or too little,
and has other faults, partly due, apparently, to recent military
organisation, partly to the feverish and unsettled state of the
civilised world. But he is still brave, when he is well led; still
loyal, above all, to his "trusty chum." Every Englishman must
hope that, if Terence Mulvaney did not take the city of Lungtung Pen as described, yet he is all ready and willing so to take
it. Mr. Mulvaney is as humorous as Micky Free, but more
melancholy and more truculent. He has, perhaps, "won his
way to the mythical" already, and is not so much a soldier,
as an incarnation, not of Krishna, but of many soldierly qualities. On the other hand, Private Ortheris, especially in his
frenzy, seems to shew all the truth, and much more than the
life of, a photograph. Such, we presume, is the soldier, and
such are his experiences and temptations and repentance. But
nobody ever dreamed of telling us all this, till Mr. Kipling came.

As for the soldier in action, the "Taking of Lungtung Pen," and the "Drums of the Fore and Aft," and that other tale of the battle with the Pathans in the gorge, are among the good fights of fiction. They stir the spirit, and they should be distributed (in addition, of course, to the "Soldier's Pocket Book") in the ranks of the British army. Mr. Kipling is as well informed about the soldier's women-kind as about the soldier: about Dinah Shadd as about Terence Mulvaney. Leaver never instructed us on these matters: Micky Free, if he loves, rides away; but Terence Mulvaney is true to his old woman. Gallant, loyal, reckless, vain, swaggering, and tender-hearted, Terence Mulvaney, if there were enough of him, "would take St. Petersburg in his drawers." Can we be too grateful to an author who has extended, as Mr. Kipling in his military sketches has extended, the frontiers of our knowledge and sympathy?

It is a mere question of individual taste; but, for my own part, had I to make a small selection from Mr. Kipling's tales, I would include more of his studies in Black than in White, and many of his excursions beyond the probable and natural. It is difficult to have one special favourite in this kind; but perhaps the story of the two English adventurers among the freemasons of unknown Kafiristan (in the "Phantom Rickshaw") would take a very high place. The gas-heated air of the Indian newspaper office is so real, and into it comes a wanderer who has seen new faces of death, and who carries with him a head that has worn a royal crown. The contrasts are of brutal force; the legend is among the best of such strange fancies. Then there is, in the same volume, "The Strange Ride of Morrowbie Jukes," the most dreadful nightmare of the most awful Bunker in the realms of fancy. This is a very early work; if nothing else of Mr. Kipling's existed, his memory might live by it, as does the memory of the American Irishman by the "Diamond Lens." The sham magic of "In the House of Suddhu" is as terrible as true necromancy could be, and I have a *faiblesse* for the "Bisara of Pooree." "The Gate of the Hundred Sorrows" is a realistic version of "The English Opium Eater," and more powerful by dint of less rhetoric. As for the sketches of native life—for example, "On the City Wall"—to English readers they are no less than revelations. They testify, more even than the military stories, to the author's swift and certain vision, his certainty in his effects. In brief, Mr. Kipling has conquered worlds, of which, as it were, we knew not the existence.

His faults are so conspicuous, so much on the surface, that they hardly need to be named. They are curiously visible to some readers who are blind to his merits. There is a false air of hardness (quite in contradiction to the sentiment in his tales of childish life); there is a knowing air; there are mannerisms, such as "But that is another story"; there is a display of slang; there is the too obtrusive knocking of the nail on the head. Everybody can mark these errors; a few cannot overcome their antipathy, and so lose a great deal of pleasure.

It is impossible to guess how Mr. Kipling will fare if he ventures on one of the usual novels, of the orthodox length. Few men have succeeded both in the *conte* and the novel. Mr. Bret Harte is limited to the *conte*; M. Guy de Maupassant is probably at his best in it. Scott wrote but three or four short tales, and only one of these is a masterpiece. Poe never attempted a novel. Hawthorne is almost alone in his command of both kinds. We can live only in the hope that Mr. Kipling, so skilled in so many species of the *conte*, so vigorous in so many kinds of verse, will also be triumphant in the novel: though it seems unlikely that its scene can be in England, and though it is certain that a writer who so cuts to the quick will not be happy with the novel's almost inevitable "padding." Mr. Kipling's longest effort, "The Light which Failed," can, perhaps, hardly be considered a test or touchstone of his powers as a novelist. The central interest is not powerful enough; the characters are not so sympathetic, as are the interest and the characters of his short pieces. Many of these persons we have met so often that they are not mere passing acquaintances, but already find in us the loyalty due to old friends.

Oscar Wilde

from *The True Function and Value of Criticism**

. . . HE WHO WOULD stir us now by fiction must either give us an entirely new background or reveal to us the soul of man in its innermost workings. The first is for the moment being done for us by Mr. Rudyard Kipling. As one turns over the pages of his *Plain Tales from the Hills,* one feels as if one were seated under a palm-tree reading life by superb flashes of vulgarity. The jaded, second-rate Anglo-Indians are in exquisite incongruity with their surroundings. The mere lack of style in the story-teller gives an odd journalistic realism to what he tells us. From the point of view of literature Mr. Kipling is a genius who drops his aspirates. From the point of view of life, he is a reporter who knows vulgarity better than any one has ever known it. Dickens knew its clothes and its comedy. Mr. Kipling knows its essence and its seriousness. He is our first authority on the second-rate, and has seen marvelous things through keyholes, and his backgrounds are real works of art.

"AN ANGLO-INDIAN'S COMPLAINT" †

To the Editor of the *Times.*
Sir,—The writer of a letter signed 'An Indian Civilian' that appears in your issue of today makes a statement about me which I beg you to allow me to correct at once.

---

* [First published in *The Nineteenth Century* in September, 1891, and reprinted with some alterations a year later in *Intentions.*]
 † [First published in *The Times,* September 25, 1891.]

7

He says that I have described the Anglo-Indians as being vulgar. This is not the case. Indeed, I have never met a vulgar Anglo-Indian. There may be many, but those whom I have had the pleasure of meeting here have been chiefly scholars, men interested in art and thought, men of cultivation; nearly all of them have been exceedingly brilliant talkers; some of them have been exceedingly brilliant writers.

What I did say—I believe in the pages of the *Nineteenth Century*—was that vulgarity is the distinguishing note of those Anglo-Indians whom Mr. Rudyard Kipling loves to write about, and writes about so cleverly. This is quite true, and there is no reason why Mr. Rudyard Kipling should not select vulgarity as his subject-matter, or as part of it. For a realistic artist, certainly, vulgarity is a most admirable subject. How far Mr. Kipling's stories really mirror Anglo-Indian society I have no idea at all, nor, indeed, am I ever much interested in any correspondence between art and nature. It seems to me a matter of entirely secondary importance. I do not wish, however, that it should be supposed that I was passing a harsh and *saugrenu* judgment on an important and in many ways distinguished class, when I was merely pointing out the characteristic qualities of some puppets in a prose-play.

I remain, Sir, your obedient servant,

Oscar Wilde.

Henry James

[The Young Kipling]*

IT WOULD BE difficult to answer the general question whether
the books of the world grow, as they multiply, as much better
as one might suppose they ought, with such a lesson on waste-
ful experiment spread perpetually behind them. There is no
doubt, however, that in one direction we profit largely by this
education: whether or no we have become wiser to fashion, we
have certainly become keener to enjoy. We have acquired the
sense of a particular quality which is precious beyond all others
—so precious as to make us wonder where, at such a rate, our
posterity will look for it, and how they will pay for it. After
tasting many essences we find freshness the sweetest of all.
We yearn for it, we watch for it and lie in wait for it, and
when we catch it on the wing (it flits by so fast), we
celebrate our capture with extravagance. We feel that
after so much has come and gone it is more and more of
a feat and a *tour de force* to be fresh. The tormenting part of
the phenomenon is that, in any particular key, it can happen
but once—by a sad failure of the law that inculcates the repetition of goodness. It is terribly a matter of accident; emulation
and imitation have a fatal effect upon it. It is easy to see, therefore, what importance the epicure may attach to the brief
moment of its bloom. While that lasts we all are epicures.
  This helps to explain, I think, the unmistakable intensity of

* [Introduction to Kipling's *Mine Own People* (New York, 1891).
Reprinted by permission of John Farquarson, Ltd.]

9

the general relish for Mr. Rudyard Kipling. His bloom lasts, from month to month, almost suprisingly—by which I mean that he has not worn out even by active exercise the particular property that made us all, more than a year ago, so precipitately drop everything else to attend to him. He has many others which he will doubtless always keep; but a part of the potency attaching to his freshness, what makes it as exciting as a drawing of lots, is our instinctive conviction that he cannot, in the nature of things, keep that; so that our enjoyment of him, so long as the miracle is still wrought, has both the charm of confidence and the charm of suspense. And then there is the further charm, with Mr. Kipling, that this same freshness is such a very strange affair of its kind—so mixed and various and cynical, and, in certain lights, so contradictory of itself. The extreme recentness of his inspiration is as enviable as the tale is startling that his productions tell of his being at home, domesticated and initiated, in this wicked and weary world. At times he strikes us as shockingly precocious, at others as serenely wise. On the whole, he presents himself as a strangely clever youth who has stolen the formidable mask of maturity and rushes about making people jump with the deep sounds, the sportive exaggerations of tone, that issue from its painted lips. He has this mark of a real vocation, that different spectators may like him—must like him, I should almost say—for different things; and this refinement of attraction, that to those who reflect even upon their pleasures he has as much to say as to those who never reflect upon anything. Indeed there is a certain amount of room for surprise in the fact that, being so much the sort of figure that the hardened critic likes to meet, he should also be the sort of figure that inspires the multitude with confidence—for a complicated air is, in general, the last thing that does this.

By the critic who likes to meet such a bristling adventurer as Mr. Kipling I mean of course the critic for whom the happy accident of character, whatever form it may take, is more of a bribe to interest than the promise of some character cherished in theory—the appearance of justifying some foregone conclusion as to what a writer or a book "ought," in the Ruskinian sense, to be; the critic in a word, who has, *à priori*, no rule for a literary production but that it shall have genuine life. Such a critic (he gets much more out of his opportunities, I think, than the other sort,) likes a writer exactly in proportion as he is a challenge, an appeal to interpretation, intelligence, ingenuity, to what is elastic in the critical mind—in proportion indeed as he may be a negation of things familiar and taken for granted. He feels in this case how much more play and sensation there is for himself.

Mr. Kipling, then, has the character that furnishes plenty of play and of vicarious experience—that makes any perceptive reader foresee a rare luxury. He has the great merit of being a compact and convenient illustration of the surest source of interest in any painter of life—that of having an identity as marked as a windowframe. He is one of the illustrations, taken near at hand, that help to clear up the vexed question, in the novel or the tale, of kinds, camps, schools, distinctions, the right way and the wrong way; so very positively does he contribute to the showing that there are just as many kinds, as many ways, as many forms and degrees of the "right," as there are personal points of view. It is the blessing of the art he practises that it is made up of experience conditioned, infinitely, in this personal way—the sum of the feeling of life as reproduced by innumerable natures; natures that feel through all their differences, testify through their diversities. These differences, which make the identity, are of the individual; they form the channel by which life flows through him, and how much he is able to give us of life—in other words, how much he appeals to us—depends on whether they form it solidly.

This hardness of the conduit, cemented with a rare assurance, is perhaps the most striking idiosyncrasy of Mr. Kipling; and what makes it more remarkable is that accident of his extreme youth which, if we talk about him at all, we cannot affect to ignore. I cannot pretend to give a biography or a chronology of the author of "Soldiers Three," but I cannot overlook the general, the importunate fact that, confidently as he has caught the trick and habit of this sophisticated world, he has not been long of it. His extreme youth is indeed what I may call his window-bar—the support on which he somewhat rowdily leans while he looks down at the human scene with his pipe in his teeth: just as his other conditions (to mention only some of them), are his prodigious facility, which is only less remarkable than his stiff selection; his unabashed temperament, his flexible talent, his smoking-room manner, his familiar friendship with India—established so rapidly, and so completely under his control; his delight in battle, his "cheek" about women—and indeed about men and about everything; his determination not to be duped, his "imperial" fibre, his love of the inside view, the private soldier and the primitive man. I must add further to this list of attractions the remarkable way in which he makes us aware that he has been put up to the whole thing directly by life (miraculously, in his teens), and not by the communications of others. These elements, and many more, constitute a singularly robust little literary character (our use of the diminutive is altogether a note of endearment and enjoyment), which, if it has the rattle of high spirits and is in no degree apologetic or shrinking, yet offers a very liberal pledge in the way of good faith and immediate performance. Mr. Kipling's performance comes off before the more circumspect have time to decide whether they like him or not, and if you have seen it once you will be sure to return to the show. He makes us prick up our ears to the good news that in the smoking-room too there may be artists; and indeed to an intimation still more refined—that the latest development of the modern also may be, most successfully, for the canny artist to put his victim off the guard by imitating the amateur (superficially, of course) to the life.

These, then, are some of the reasons why Mr. Kipling may be dear to the analyst as well as, M. Renan says, to the simple. The simple may like him because he is wonderful about India, and India has not been "done"; while there is plenty left for the morbid reader in the surprise of his skill and the *fioriture* of his form, which are so oddly independent of any distinctively literary note in him, any bookish association. It is as one of the morbid that the writer of these remarks (which doubtless only too shamefully betray his character) exposes himself as most consentingly under the spell. The freshness arising from a subject that—by a good fortune I do not mean

to under-estimate—has never been "done," is after all less of
an affair to build upon than the freshness residing in the
temper of the artist. Happy indeed is Mr. Kipling, who can
command so much of both kinds. It is still as one of the
morbid, no doubt—that is, as one of those who are capable
of sitting up all night for a new impression of talent, of
scouring the trodden field for one little spot of green—that I
find our young author quite most curious in his air, and
not only in his air but in his evidently very real sense, of
knowing his way about life. Curious in the highest degree and
well worth attention is such an idiosyncrasy as this in a young
Anglo-Saxon. We meet it with familiar frequency in the bud-
ding talents of France, and it startles and haunts us for an
hour. After an hour, however, the mystery is apt to fade, for
we find that the wondrous initiation is not in the least general, is only exceedingly special, and is, even with this limita-
tion, very often rather conventional. In a word, it is with the
ladies that the young Frenchman takes his ease, and more
particularly with ladies selected expressly to make this attitude convincing. When *they* have let him off, the dimnesses
too often encompass him. But for Mr. Kipling there are no
dimnesses anywhere, and if the ladies are indeed violently
distinct they are only strong notes in a universal loudness.
This loudness fills the ears of Mr. Kipling's admirers (it lacks
sweetness, no doubt, for those who are not of the number),
and there is really only one strain that is absent from it—the
voice, as it were, of the civilised man; in whom I of course
also include the civilised woman. But this is an element that
for the present one does not miss—every other note is so
articulate and direct.

It is a part of the satisfaction the author gives us that he
can make us speculate as to whether he will be able to complete his picture altogether (this is as far as we presume
to go in meddling with the question of his future) without
bringing in the complicated soul. On the day he does so, if
he handles it with anything like the cleverness he has already
shown, the expectation of his friends will take a great bound.
Meanwhile, at any rate, we have Mulvaney, and Mulvaney is
after all tolerably complicated. He is only a six-foot saturated

Irish private, but he is a considerable pledge of more to come. Hasn't he, for that matter, the tongue of a hoarse syren, and hasn't he also mysteries and infinitudes almost Carlylese? Since I am speaking of him I may as well say that, as an evocation, he has probably led captive those of Mr. Kipling's readers who have most given up resistance. He is a piece of portraiture of the largest, vividest kind, growing and growing on the painter's hands without ever outgrowing them. I can't help regarding him, in a certain sense, as Mr. Kipling's tutelary deity—a landmark in the direction in which it is open to him to look furthest. If the author will only go as far in this direction as Mulvaney is capable of taking him (and the inimitable Irishman is, like Voltaire's Habakkuk, *capable de tout*), he may still discover a treasure and find a reward for the services he has rendered the winner of Dinah Shadd. I hasten to add that the truly appreciative reader should surely have no quarrel with the primitive element in Mr. Kipling's subject-matter, or with what, for want of a better name, I may call his love of low life. What is that but essentially a part of his freshness? And for what part of his freshness are we exactly more thankful than for just this smart jostle that he gives the old stupid superstition that the amiability of a storyteller is the amiability of the people he represents—that their vulgarity, or depravity, or gentility, or fatuity are tantamount to the same qualities in the painter himself? A blow from which, apparently, it will not easily recover is dealt this infantine philosophy by Mr. Howells when, with the most distinguished dexterity and all the detachment of a master, he handles some of the clumsiest, crudest, most human things in life—answering surely thereby the playgoers in the sixpenny gallery who howl at the representative of the villain when he comes before the curtain.

Nothing is more refreshing than this active, disinterested sense of the real; it is doubtless the quality for the want of more of which our English and American fiction has turned so woefully stale. We are ridden by the old conventionalities of type and small proprieties of observance—by the foolish babyformula (to put it sketchily) of the picture and the subject. Mr. Kipling has all the air of being disposed to lift the whole business off the nursery carpet, and of being perhaps even more able than he is disposed. One must hasten of course to parenthesise that there is not, intrinsically, a bit more luminosity in treating of low life and of primitive man than of those whom civilisation has kneaded to a finer paste: the only luminosity in either case is in the intelligence with which the thing is done. But it so happens that, among ourselves, the frank, capable outlook, when turned upon the vulgar majority, the coarse, receding edges of the social perspective, borrows a charm from being new; such a charm as, for instance, repetition has already despoiled it of among the French—the hapless French who pay the penalty as well as enjoy the glow of living intellectually so much faster than we. It is the most inexorable part of our fate that we grow tired of everything, and of course in due time we may grow tired even of what explorers shall come back to tell us about the great grimy condition, or, with unprecedented items and details, about the grey middle state which darkens into it. But the explorers, bless them! may have a long day before that; it is early to trouble about reactions, so that we must give them the benefit of every presumption. We are thankful for any boldness and any sharp curiosity, and that is why we are thankful for Mr. Kipling's general spirit and for most of his excursions.

Many of these, certainly, are into a region not to be designated as superficially dim, though indeed the author always reminds us that India is above all the land of mystery. A large part of his high spirits, and of ours, comes doubtless from the amusement of such vivid, heterogeneous material, from the irresistible magic of scorching suns, subject empires, uncanny religions, uneasy garrisons and smothered-up women—from heat and colour and danger and dust. India is a portentous image, and we are duly awed by the familiarities it undergoes at Mr. Kipling's hands and by the fine impunity, the sort of fortune that favours the brave, of *his* want of awe. An abject humility is not his strong point, but he gives us something instead of it—vividness and drollery, the vision and the thrill of many things, the misery and strangeness of most, the personal sense of a hundred queer contacts and risks. And then in the absence of respect he has plenty of knowledge, and if knowledge should fail him he would have plenty of invention. Moreover, if invention should ever fail him, he would still have the lyric string and the patriotic chord, on which he plays admirably; so that it may be said he is a man of resources. What he gives us, above all, is the feeling of the English manner and the English blood in conditions they have made at once so much and so little their own; with manifestations grotesque enough in some of his satiric sketches and deeply impressive in some of his anecdotes of individual responsibility.

His Indian impressions divide themselves into three groups, one of which, I think, very much outshines the others. First to be mentioned are the tales of native life, curious glimpses of custom and superstition, dusky matters not beholden of the many, for which the author has a remarkable *flair*. Then comes the social, the Anglo-Indian episode, the study of administrative and military types and of the wonderful rattling, riding ladies who, at Simla and more desperate stations, look out for husbands and lovers; often, it would seem, the husbands and lovers of others. The most brilliant group is devoted wholly to the common soldier, and of this series it appears to me that too much good is hardly to be said. Here Mr. Kipling, with all his offhandness, is a master; for we are held not so much by the greater or less oddity of the particular yarn—sometimes it is scarcely a yarn at all, but something much less artificial—as by the robust attitude of the narrator, who never arranges or glosses or falsifies, but makes straight for the common and the characteristic. I have mentioned the great esteem in which I hold Mulvaney—surely a charming man and one qualified to adorn a higher sphere. Mulvaney is a creation to be proud of, and his two comrades stand as firm on their legs. In spite of Mulvaney's social possibilities they are all three finished brutes; but it is precisely in the finish that we delight. Whatever Mr. Kipling may relate about them for ever will encounter readers equally fascinated and unable fully to justify their faith.

Are not those literary pleasures after all the most intense which are the most perverse and whimsical, and even indefensible? There is a logic in them somewhere, but it often lies below the plummet of criticism. The spell may be weak in a writer who has every reasonable and regular claim, and it may be irresistible in one who presents himself with a style corresponding to a bad hat. A good hat is better than a bad one, but a conjurer may wear either. Many a reader will never be able to say what secret human force lays its hand upon him when Private Ortheris, having sworn "quietly into the blue sky," goes mad with home-sickness by the yellow river and raves for the basest sights and sounds of London. I can scarcely tell why I think "The Courting of Dinah Shadd" a masterpiece (though, indeed, I can make a shrewd guess at one of the reasons), nor would it be worth while perhaps to attempt to defend the same pretension in regard to "On Greenhow Hill"—much less to trouble the tolerant reader of these remarks with a statement of how many more performances in the nature of "The End of the Passage" (quite admitting even that they might not represent Mr. Kipling at his best), I am conscious of a latent relish for. One might as well admit while one is about it that one has wept profusely over "The Drums of the Fore and Aft," the history of the "Dutch courage" of two dreadful dirty little boys, who, in the face of Afghans scarcely more dreadful, saved the reputation of their regiment and perished, the least mawkishly in the world, in a squalor of battle incomparably expressed. People who know how peaceful they are themselves and have no bloodshed to reproach themselves with needn't scruple to mention the glamour that Mr. Kipling's intense militarism has for them and how astonishing and contagious they find it, in spite of the unromantic complexion of it—the way it bristles with all sorts of uglinesses and technicalities. Perhaps that is why I go all the way even with "The Gadsbys"—the Gadsbys were so connected (uncomfortably it is true) with the Army. There is fearful fighting—or a fearful danger of it— in "The Man who would be King": is that the reason we are deeply affected by this extraordinary tale? It is one of them, doubtless, for Mr. Kipling has many reasons, after all, on his side, though they don't equally call aloud to be uttered.

One more of them, at any rate, I must add to these unsystematised remarks—it is the one I spoke of a shrewd guess at in alluding to "The Courting of Dinah Shadd." The talent

that produces such a tale is a talent eminently in harmony
with the short story, and the short story is, on our side of
the Channel and of the Atlantic, a mine which will take a
great deal of working. Admirable is the clearness with which
Mr. Kipling perceives this—perceives what innumerable chances
it gives, chances of touching life in a thousand different places,
taking it up in innumerable pieces, each a specimen and an
illustration. In a word, he appreciates the episode, and there
are signs to show that this shrewdness will, in general, have
long innings. It will find the detachable, compressible "case"
an admirable, flexible form; the cultivation of which may well
add to the mistrust already entertained by Mr. Kipling, if his
manner does not betray him, for what is clumsy and tasteless
in the time-honoured practice of the "plot." It will fortify
him in the conviction that the vivid picture has a greater
communicative value than the Chinese puzzle. There is little
enough "plot" in such a perfect little piece of hard representation as "The End of the Passage," to cite again only the most
salient of twenty examples.

But I am speaking of our author's future, which is the luxury
that I meant to forbid myself—precisely because the subject
is so tempting. There is nothing in the world (for the prophet)
so charming as to prophesy, and as there is nothing so inconclusive the tendency should be repressed in proportion as
the opportunity is good. There is a certain want of courtesy
to a peculiarly contemporaneous present even in speculating,
with a dozen deferential precautions, on the question of what
will become in the later hours of the day of a talent that has
got up so early. Mr. Kipling's actual performance is like a
tremendous walk before breakfast, making one welcome the
idea of the meal, but consider with some alarm the hours
still to be traversed. Yet if his breakfast is all to come the
indications are that he will be more active than ever after he
has had it. Among these indications are the unflagging character of his pace and the excellent form, as they say in athletic
circles, in which he gets over the ground. We don't detect him
stumbling; on the contrary, he steps out quite as briskly as at
first and still more firmly. There is something zealous and
craftsman-like in him which shows that he feels both joy and

responsibility. A whimsical, wanton reader, haunted by a recollection of all the good things he has seen spoiled; by a sense of the miserable, or, at any rate, the inferior, in so many continuations and endings, is almost capable of perverting poetic justice to the idea that it would be even positively well for so surprising a producer to remain simply the fortunate, suggestive, unconfirmed and unqualified representative of what he has actually done. We can always refer to that.

Robert Buchanan

from *The Voice of The Hooligan**

. . . NOW THAT Mr. Gladstone has departed, we possess no politician, with the single exception of Mr. Morley (whose sanity and honesty are unquestionable, though he lacks, unfortunately, the dæmonic influence), who demands for the discussion of public affairs any conscientious and unselfish sanction whatever; we possess, instead, a thousand pertinacious counsellors, cynics like Lord Salisbury or trimmers like Lord Rosebery, for whom no one in his heart of hearts feels the slightest respect. Our fashionable society is admittedly so rotten, root and branch, that not even the queen's commanding influence can impart to it the faintest suggestion of purity, or even decency. As for our popular literature, it has been in many of its manifestations long past praying for; it has run to seed in fiction of the baser sort, seldom or never, with all its cleverness, touching the quick of human conscience; but its most extraordinary feature at this moment is the exaltation to a position of almost unexampled popularity of a writer who in his single person adumbrates, I think, all that is most deplorable, all that is most retrograde and savage, in the restless and uninstructed Hooliganism of the time.

The English public's first knowledge of Mr. Rudyard Kipling was gathered from certain brief anecdotal stories and occasional

---

* [From *The Voice of "The Hooligan"*: *A Discussion of Kiplingism* (New York, 1900). A number of long passages dealing with the general condition of England have been omitted here. Everything which Buchanan had to say about Kipling has been retained.]

verses which began to be quoted about a decade ago in England, and which were speedily followed by cheap reprints of the originals, sold on every bookstall. They possessed one not inconsiderable attraction, in so far as they dealt with a naturally romantic country, looming very far off to English readers, and doubly interesting as one of our own great national possessions. We had had many works about India—works of description and works of fiction; and a passionate interest in them, and in all that pertained to things Anglo-Indian, had been awakened by the Mutiny; but few writers had dealt with the ignobler details of military and civilian life, with the gossip of the mess-room and the scandal of the governmental departments. Mr. Kipling's little kodak-glimpses, therefore, seemed unusually fresh and new; nor would it be just to deny them the merits of great liveliness, intimate personal knowledge, and a certain unmistakable, though obviously cockney, humor. Although they dealt almost entirely with the baser aspects of our civilization, being chiefly devoted to the affairs of idle military men, savage soldiers, frisky wives and widows, and flippant civilians, they were indubitably bright and clever, and in the background of them we perceived, faintly but distinctly, the shadow of the great and wonderful national life of India. At any rate, whatever their merits were—and I hold their merits to be indisputable—they became rapidly popular, especially with the newspaper press, which hailed the writer as a new and quite amazing force in literature. So far as the lazy public was concerned, they had the one delightful merit of extreme brevity; he that ran might read them, just as he read "Tid-bits" and the society newspapers, and then treat them like the rose in Browning's poem:

> Smell, kiss, wear it,—at last throw away!

Two factors contributed to their vogue: first, the utter apathy of general readers, too idle and uninstructed to study works of any length or demanding any contribution of serious thought on the reader's part, and eager for any amusement which did not remind them of the eternal problems which once beset humanity; and, second, the rapid growth in every direction of the military or militant spirit, of the Primrose League, of aggression abroad, and indifference at home to all religious ideals—in a word, of Greater Englandism, or Imperialism. For a considerable time Mr. Kipling poured out a rapid succession of these little tales and smoking-room anecdotes, to the great satisfaction of those who loved to listen to banalities about the English flag, seasoned with strong suggestions of social impropriety, as revealed in camps and barracks and the boudoirs of officers' mistresses and wives. The things seem harmless enough, if not very elevating or ennobling. Encouraged by his success, the author attempted longer flights, with very indifferent results; though in the "Jungle Books," for example, he got near to a really imaginative presentment of fine material, and, if he had continued his work in that direction, criticism might have had little or nothing to say against him. But in an unfortunate moment, encouraged by the journalistic praise lavished on certain fragments of verse with which he had ornamented his prose effusions, he elected to challenge criticism as a poet—as, indeed, the approved and authoritative poet of the British empire; and the first result of this election, or, as I prefer to call it, this delusion and hallucination, was the publication of the volume of poems, partly new and partly reprinted, called "Barrack-Room Ballads."

I have said that Mr. Kipling's estimate of himself as a poet was a delusion; it was no delusion, however, so far as his faith in the public was concerned. The book was received with instantaneous and clamorous approval; and, once again, let me pause to admit that it contained, here and there, glimpses of a real verse-making faculty—a faculty which, had the writer been spiritually and intellectually equipped, might have led to the production of work entitled to be called "poetry." On the very first page, however, the note of insincerity was struck, in a dedication addressed to Mr. Wolcott Balestier, but recognized at once as having done duty for quite a different purpose—resembling in this respect the famous acrostic of Mr. Slum, which, although written to fit the name of "Warren," —became at a pinch "a positive inspiration for Jarley." This dedication, with its false feeling and utterly unsuitable imagery, suggests the remark en passant that Mr. Kipling's muse alternates between two extremes—the lowest cockney vulgarity

and the very height of what Americans call "high-falutin'"—
so that, when it is not setting the teeth on edge with the
vocabulary of the London Hooligan, it is raving in capital letters about the Seraphim and the Pit and the Maidens Nine
and the Planets.

The "Ballads" thus introduced are twenty-one in number,
of which the majority are descriptive of whatever is basest
and most brutal in the character of the British mercenary.
One deals, naturally enough, with the want of sympathy shown
in public-houses to Tommie Atkins in time of peace, as contrasted with the enthusiasm for him in time of war; another,
entitled "Cells," begins as follows:

I've a head like a concertina: I've a tongue like a button-stick:
I've a mouth like an old potato, and I'm more than a little sick.
But I've had my fun with the Corp'ral's Guard: I've made the
   cinders fly,
And I'm here in the Clink for a thundering drink and blacking the
   Corp'ral's eye;

it is, in fact, the glorification of the familiar episode of "drunk
and resisting the guard." In an equally sublime spirit is conceived the ballad called "Loot," beginning:

If you've ever stole a pheasant-egg be-'ind the keeper's back,
   If you've even snigged the washin' from a line,
If you've ever crammed a gander in your bloomin' 'aversack,
   You will understand this little song of mine;

and the verses are indeed, with their brutal violence and their
hideous refrain, only too sadly understandable. Worse still,
in its horrible savagery, is the piece called "Belts," which is
the apotheosis of the soldier who uses his belt in drunken fury
to assault civilians in the streets, and which has this agreeable
refrain:

But it was: "Belts, belts, belts, an' that's one for you!"
An' it was "Belts, belts, belts, an' that's done for you!"
         O buckle an' tongue
         Was the song that we sung
From Harrison's down to the Park!

If it is suggested that the poems I have quoted are only
incidental bits of local color, interspersed among verses of a

very different character, the reply is that those pieces, although they are certainly the least defensible, are quite in keeping with the other ballads, scarcely one of which reaches to the intellectual level of the lowest music-hall effusions. The best of them is a ballad called "Mandalay," and describing the feelings of a soldier who regrets the heroine of a little amour out in India, and it certainly possesses a real melody and a certain pathos. But in all the ballads, with scarcely an exception, the tone is one of absolute vulgarity and triviality, unredeemed by a touch of human tenderness and pity. Even the little piece called "Soldier, Soldier," which begins quite naturally and tenderly, ends with the cynical suggestion that the lady who mourns her old love had better take up at once with the party who brings the news of his death:

> True love! new love!
> Best take 'im for a new love!
> The dead they cannot rise, an' you'd better dry your eyes,
> An' you'd best take 'im for your true love.

With such touching sweetness and tender verisimilitude are these ballads of the barrack filled from end to end. Seriously, the picture they present is one of unmitigated barbarism. The Tommie Atkins they introduce is a drunken, swearing, coarse-minded Hooligan, for whom, nevertheless, our sympathy is eagerly entreated. Yet these pieces were accepted on their publication, not as a cruel libel on the British soldier, but as a perfect and splendid representation of the red-coated patriot on whom our national security chiefly depended, and who was spreading abroad in every country the glory of our imperial flag!

That we might be in no doubt about the sort of thinker who was claiming our suffrages, Mr. Kipling printed at the end of his book certain other lyrics not specially devoted to the military. The best of these, the "Ballad of the *Bolivar*," is put into the mouth of seven drunken sailors "rolling down the Ratcliffe Road drunk and raising Cain," and loudly proclaiming, with the true brag and bluster so characteristic of modern British heroism, how "they took the (water-logged) *Bolivar* across the Bay." It seems, by the way, a favorite condition with Mr. Kipling, when he celebrates acts of manly daring, that his subjects should be mad drunk, and, at any rate, as drunken in their language as possible. But this ballad may pass, that we may turn to the poem "Cleared," in which Mr. Kipling spits all the venom of cockney ignorance on the Irish party, *a propos* of a certain Commission of which we have all heard, and, while saying nothing on the subject of forged letters and cowardly accusations, affirms that Irish patriots are naturally and distinctively murderers, because in the name of patriotism murders have now and then been done. He who loves blood and gore so much, who cannot even follow the soldier home into our streets without celebrating his drunken assaults and savageries, has only hate and loathing for the unhappy nation which has suffered untold wrong, and which, when all is said and done, has struck back so seldom. In the poem which follows, "An Imperial Rescript," he protests with all his might against any bond of brotherhood among the sons of toil, pledging the strong to work for and help the weak. Here, as elsewhere, he is on the side of all that is ignorant, selfish, base, and brutal in the instincts of humanity.

Before proceeding further to estimate Mr. Kipling's contributions to literature, let me glance for a moment at his second book of verse, "The Seven Seas," published a year or two ago. It may be granted at once that it was a distinct advance on its predecessor, more restrained, less vulgar, and much more varied; here and there, indeed, as in the opening "Song of the English," it struck a note of distinct and absolute poetry. But, in spite of its unquestionable picturesqueness, and of a certain swing and lilt in the go-as-you-please rhythms, it was still characterized by the same indefinable quality of brutality and latent baseness. Many of the poems, such as the "Song of the Banjo," were on the level of the cleverness to be found in the contributions of the poet of the "Sporting Times," known to the occult as the "Pink 'Un." The large majority, indeed, were cockney in spirit, in language, and in inspiration, and one or two, such as "The Ladies" and "The Sergeant's Weddin'," with its refrain:

> Cheer for the Sergeant's weddin'—
> Give 'em one cheer more!
> Grey gun-'orses in the lando,
> And a rogue is married to etc.,

were frankly and brutally indecent. The army appeared again, in the same ignoble light as before, with the same disregard of all literary luxuries, even of grammar and the aspirate. God, too, loomed largely in these productions, a cockney "Gawd" again, chiefly requisitioned for purposes of blasphemy and furious emphasis. There was no glimpse anywhere of sober and self-respecting human beings—only a wild carnival of drunken, bragging, boasting Hooligans in red coats and seamen's jackets, shrieking to the sound of the banjo and applauding the English flag. . . .

Turning over the leaves of [Mr. Kipling's] poems, one is transported at once to the region of low drinking-dens and gin-palaces, of dirty dissipation and drunken brawls; and the voice we hear is always the voice of the soldier whose God is a cockney "Gawd," and who is ignorant of the aspirate in either heaven or hell. Are there no Scotchmen in the ranks, no Highlanders, no men from Dublin or Tipperary, no Lancashire or Yorkshire men, no Welshmen, and no men of any kind who speak the Queen's English? It would seem not, if the poet of "The Sergeant's Weddin'" is to be trusted. Nor have our mercenaries, from the ranks upwards, any one thing, except brute courage, to distinguish them from the beasts of the field. This, at least, appears to be Mr. Kipling's contention, and even in the Service itself it seems to be undisputed.

How, then, are we to account for the extraordinary popularity of works so contemptible in spirit and so barbarous in execution? In the first place, even fairly educated readers were sick to death of the insincerities and affectations of the professional "Poets," with one or two familiar exceptions, and, failing the advent of a popular singer like Burns, capable of setting to brisk music the simple joys and sorrows of humanity, they turned eagerly to any writer who wrote verse, doggerel even, which seemed thoroughly alive. They were amused, therefore, by the free-and-easy rattles, the jog-trot tunes, which had hitherto been heard only in the music-halls and read only in the sporting newspapers. In the second place, the spirit abroad to-day is the spirit of ephemeral journalism, and whatever accords with that spirit—its vulgarity, its flippancy, and its radical unintelligence—is certain to attain tremendous vogue. Anything that demands a moment's thought or a moment's severe attention, anything that is not thoroughly noisy, blatant, cocksure, and self-assertive, is *caviare* to that man in the street on whom cheap journalism depends, and who, it should be said *en passant*, is often a member of smart society. In the third place, Mr. Kipling had the good, or bad, fortune to come at the very moment when the wave of false Imperialism was cresting most strongly upward, and when even the great organs of opinion, organs which, like the "Times," subsist entirely on the good or bad passions of the hour, were in sore need of a writer who could express in fairly readable numbers the secret yearnings and sympathies of the baser military and commercial spirit. Mr. Kipling, in a word, although not a poet at all in the true sense of the word, is as near an approach to a poet as can be tolerated by the ephemeral and hasty judgment of the day. His very incapacity of serious thought or deep feeling is in his favor. He represents, with more or less accuracy, what the mob is thinking, and for this very reason he is likely to be forgotten as swiftly and summarily as he has been applauded, nay, to be judged and condemned as mean and insignificant on grounds quite as hasty as those on which he has been hailed as important and high-minded. Savage animalism and ignorant vain-glory being in the ascendant, he is hailed at every street-corner and crowned by every newspaper. To-morrow, when the wind changes, and the silly crowd is in another and possibly saner temper, he is certain to fare very differently. The misfortune is that his effusions have no real poetical quality to preserve them when their momentary purpose has been served. Of more than one poet of this generation it has been said that "he uttered nothing base." Of Mr. Kipling it may be said, so far at least as his verses are concerned, that he has scarcely on any single occasion uttered anything that does not suggest moral baseness, or hover dangerously near it.

However, that we might not entertain one lingering doubt as to the nature of the spirit which inspires his easy-going muse, Mr. Kipling himself, with a candor for which we cannot be sufficiently thankful, has recently laid bare, in a prose work, the inmost springs of his inspiration; in other words, he has described to us, with fearless and shameless accuracy, in a record of English boyhood, his ideal of the human character in adolescence. Now, there is nothing which so clearly and absolutely represents the nature of a grown man's intelligence as the manner in which he contemplates, looking backward, the feelings and aspirations of youthful days. "Heaven lies about us in our infancy," says the author of the immortal Ode, and heaven is still with us very often as we more closely approach to manhood. In Goethe's reminiscences of his childhood, we discover, faintly developing, all that was wisest and most beautiful in a soul which was distinguished, despite many imperfections, by an inherent love of gentleness and wisdom; the eager intelligence, the vision, the curiosity, are all there, in every thought and act of an extraordinary child. When Dickens, in "David Copperfield," described under a thin veil of fiction the joys and sorrows of his own boyhood and youth, there welled up out of his great heart a love, a tenderness, a humor which filled the eyes of all humanity with happy tears. When Thackeray touched the same chords, as he did more than once, he was no longer the glorified Jeames of latter-day fiction—he was as kindly, as tender, and as loving as even his great contemporary. Even George Eliot, with imaginative gifts so far inferior, reached the height of her artistic achievement when she went back to the emotions of her early days— when, for example, she described the personal relations of Tom and Maggie Tulliver, or when, in the one real poem she ever wrote, she told in sonnet-sequence of the little "Brother and Sister." It would be cruel, even brutal, to talk of Mr. Rudyard Kipling in the same breath as fine artists like these; but all writers, great or little, must finally be judged by the same test—that of the truth and beauty, the sanity or the folly, of their representations of our manifold human nature. Mere truth is not sufficient for Art; the truth must be there, but it must be spiritualized and have become beautiful. In "Stalky & Co." Mr. Kipling obviously aims at verisimilitude; the picture he draws is at any rate repulsive and disgusting enough to be true; yet I trust for England's sake that it is not—that it is, like nearly all his writings with which I am familiar, merely a savage caricature.

Only the spoiled child of an utterly brutalized public could possibly have written "Stalky & Co.," or, having written it, have dared to publish it. These are strong words, but they can be justified. The story ran originally through the pages of a cheap monthly magazine, and contained, I fancy, in its first form, certain passages which the writer himself was compelled in pure shame to suppress. Its purpose, almost openly avowed, is to furnish English readers with an antidote to what Mr. Kipling styles *Ericism,* by which label is meant the kind of "sentiment" which was once made familiar to schoolboys by Farrar's "Eric, or, Little by Little"; or, to put the matter in other words, the truly ideal schoolboy is not a little sentimentalist, he is simply a little beast. The heroes of this deplorable book are three youths, dwelling in a training school near Westward Ho!; one of them, the Beetle, reads poetry and wears spectacles, the two others, Stalky and M'Turk, are his bosom companions. This trio are leagued together for purposes of offence and defence against their comrades; they join in no honest play or manly sports, they lounge about, they drink, they smoke, they curse and swear, not like boys at all, but like hideous little men. Owing to their determination to obey their own instincts, and their diabolic ingenuity in revenging themselves on any one who meddles with them, they become a terror to the school. It is quietly suggested, however, that the head master sympathizes with them, especially in their power to inflict pain wantonly and to bear it stoically, which appears to him the noblest attribute of a human being. It is simply impossible to show by mere quotations the horrible vileness of the book describing the lives of these three small fiends in human likeness; only a perusal of the whole work would convey to the reader its truly repulsive character, and to read the pages through, I fear, would sorely test the stomach of any sensitive reader. The nature of one of the longest and most important episodes may be gathered from the statement that the episode turns on the way in which the three young Hooligans revenge themselves on a number of their schoolmates who have offended them, by means of a dead and putrefying cat. And here is a sample of the dialogue:

> In his absence not less than half the school invaded the infected dormitory to draw their own conclusions. The cat had gained in the last twelve hours, but a battlefield of the fifth day could not have been so flamboyant as the spies reported.
>
> "My word, she *is* doin' herself proud," said Stalky. "Did you ever smell anything like it? Ah, and she isn't under White's dormitory at all yet."
>
> "But she will be. Give her time," said Beetle. "She'll twine like a giddy honeysuckle. What howlin' Lazerites they are! No house is justified in makin' itself a stench in the nostrils of decent——"
>
> "High-minded, pure-souled boys. *Do* you burn with remorse and regret?" said M'Turk, as they hastened to meet the house coming up from the sea.

Another equally charming episode is the one describing how a certain plebeian called "Rabbits-Eggs," through the machinations of the trio, wrecked the room of one of the masters, King:

> "*Moi! Je! Ich! Ego!*" gasped Stalky, "I waited till I couldn't hear myself think, while you played the drum! Hid in the coal-locker and tweaked Rabbits-Eggs—and Rabbits-Eggs rocked King. Wasn't it beautiful! Did you hear the glass?"
>
> "Why, he—he—he," shrieked M'Turk, one trembling finger pointed at Beetle.
>
> "Why, I—I—I was through it all," Beetle howled; "in his study, being jawed."
>
> "Oh, my soul!" said Stalky, with a yell, disappearing under water.
>
> "The, the glass was nothing. Manders minor's head's cut open. La—la—lamp upset all over the rug. Blood on the books and papers. The gum! The gum! The gum! The ink! The ink! Oh, Lord!"
>
> Then Stalky leaped out, all pink as he was, and shook Beetle into some sort of coherence; but his tale prostrated them afresh.
>
> "I bunked for the boot-cupboard the second I heard King go down stairs. Beetle tumbled in on top of me. The spare key's hid behind the loose board. There isn't a shadow of evidence," said Stalky. They were all chanting together.
>
> "And he turned us out himself—himself—him*self!*" This from M'Turk. "He can't begin to suspect us. Oh, Stalky, it's the loveliest thing we've ever done!"
>
> "Gum! Gum! Dollops of gum!" shouted Beetle, his spectacles gleaming through a sea of lather. "Ink and blood all mixed. I held the little beast's head all over the Latin proses for Monday. Golly,

how the oil stunk! And Rabbits-Eggs told King to poultice his nose!
Did you hit Rabbits-Eggs, Stalky?"

"Did I jolly well not? Tweaked him all over. Did you hear him
curse? Oh, I shall be sick in a minute if I don't stop!"

As I have already said, however, the book cannot be represented by extracts. The vulgarity, the brutality, the savagery,
reeks on every page. It may be noted as a minor peculiarity
that everything, according to our young Hooligans, is "beastly,"
or "giddy," or "blooming"; adjectives of this sort cropping up
everywhere in their conversation, as in that of the savages of
the London slums. And the moral of the book—for, of course,
like all such banalities, it professes to have a moral—is that
out of materials like these is fashioned the humanity which
is to ennoble and preserve our Anglo-Saxon empire! "India's
full of Stalkies," says the Beetle, "Cheltenham and Haileybury
and Marlborough chaps—that we don't know anything about,
and *the surprises will begin when there is really a big row on!*"

Perhaps, after all I am unjust to Mr. Kipling in forgetting
for the moment to credit him with a poet's prophetic vision?
For, if "Stalky & Co." was written before and not after recent
political developments, it certainly furnishes a foretaste of
what has actually happened! The "surprises *have* begun," although the "rows" have not been very "big" ones, and the
souls of Stalky and his companions *have* been looming large
in our empire. Studying certain latter-day records,[1] indeed, listening to the voice of the Hooligan in politics, in literature, and
journalism, is really very like reading "Stalky & Co." Some of

[1] It is sad to read in this connection the poem contributed to the
"Times," at the outbreak of the South African struggle, by no less a per-
son than Ven. Dr. Alexander, archbishop of Armagh and primate of all
Ireland:

> They say that "War is Hell," the "great accursed,"
>   The sin impossible to be forgiven—
> Yet I can look upon it at its worst,
>   And still find blue in heaven!
>
> And, as I note how nobly natures form
>   Under the war's red rain, I deem it true
> That He who made the earthquake and the storm
>   Perchance made battles too!

God help the church, indeed, if this is the sort of oracle she delivers to
those who rested their faith in God on the message of the Beatitudes.

our battles, even, faithfully reproduce the "blooming" and
"giddy" orgies of the schoolroom, and in not a few of our public affairs there is a "stench" like that of "the dead cat." Yes,
there *must* be Stalkies and M'Turks and Beetles working busily,
after all, and representing the new spirit which appears to have
begun in the time of Mr. Kipling's boyhood. But whether they
really represent the true spirit of our civilization, and make for
its salvation, is a question which I will leave my readers to decide. . . .

Max Beerbohm

P.C., X, 36 *

> Then it's collar 'im tight,
> In the name o' the Lawd!
> 'Ustle 'im, shake 'im till 'e's sick!
> Wot, 'e *would*, would 'e? Well,
> Then yer've got ter give 'im 'Ell,
> An' it's trunch, trunch, truncheon does the trick.
>
> POLICE STATION DITTIES

I HAD SPENT Christmas Eve at the Club, listening to a grand pow-wow between certain of the choicer sons of Adam. Then Slushby had cut in. Slushby is one who writes to newspapers and is theirs obediently "HUMANITARIAN." When Slushby cuts in, men remember they have to be up early next morning.

Sharp round a corner on the way home, I collided with something firmer than the regulation pillar-box. I righted myself after the recoil and saw some stars that were very pretty indeed. Then I perceived the nature of the obstruction.

"Evening, Judlip," I said sweetly, when I had collected my hat from the gutter. "Have I broken the law, Judlip? If so, I'll go quiet."

"Time yer was in bed," grunted X, 36. "Yer Ma'll be lookin' out for yer."

This from the friend of my bosom! It hurt. Many were the night-beats I had been privileged to walk with Judlip, imbibing curious lore that made glad the civilian heart of me. Seven whole 8 x 5 inch note-books had I pitmanised to the brim with Judlip. And now to be repulsed as one of the uninitiated! It hurt horrid.

There is a thing called Dignity. Small boys sometimes stand on it. Then they have to be kicked. Then they get down, weeping. I don't stand on Dignity.

* [From A *Christmas Garland* (London, 1912), pp. 11–20. Reprinted by permission of William Heinemann, Ltd., and from A *Christmas Garland*, Dutton Paperback Edition, by permission of E. P. Dutton & Co., Inc.]

33

"What's wrong, Judlip?" I asked, more sweetly than ever. "Drawn a blank tonight?"

"Yuss. Drawn a blank blank blank. 'Aven't 'ad so much as a kick at a lorst dorg. Christmas Eve ain't wot it was." I felt for my note-book. "Lawd! I remembers the time when the drunks and disorderlies down this street was as thick as flies on a fly-paper. One just picked 'em orf with one's finger and thumb. A bloomin' battew, that's wot it wos."

"The night's yet young, Judlip," I insinuated, with a jerk of my thumb at the flaring windows of the "Rat and Blood Hound." At that moment the saloon-door swung open, emitting a man and woman who walked with linked arms and exceeding great care.

Judlip eyed them longingly as they tacked up the street. Then he sighed. Now, when Judlip sighs the sound is like unto that which issues from the vent of a Crosby boiler when the cog-gauges are at 260°F.

"Come, Judlip!" I said. "Possess your soul in patience. You'll soon find someone to make an example of. Meanwhile"—I threw back my head and smacked my lips—"the usual, Judlip?"

In another minute I emerged through the swing-door, bearing a furtive glass of that same "usual," and nipped down the mews where my friend was wont to await these little tokens of esteem.

"To the Majesty of the Law, Judlip!"

When he had honoured the toast, I scooted back with the glass, leaving him wiping the beads off his beard-bristles. He was in his philosophic mood when I rejoined him at the corner.

"Wot am I?" he said, as we paced along, "A bloomin' cypher. Wot's the sarjint? 'E's got the Inspector over 'im. Over above the Inspector there's the Sooprintendent. Over above 'im's the old red-tape-masticatin' Yard. Over above that there's the 'Ome Sec. Wot's 'e? A cypher, like me. Why?" Judlip looked up at the stars. "Over above 'im's We Dunno Wot. Somethin' wot issues its horders an' regulations an' divisional injunctions, inscrootable like, but p'remptory; an' we 'as ter see as 'ow they're carried out, not arskin' no questions, but each man goin' about 'is dooty."

"'Is dooty,'" said I, looking up from my note-book. "Yes, I've got that."

"Life ain't a bean-feast. It's a 'arsh reality. An' them as makes it a bean-feast 'as got to be 'arshly dealt with accordin'. That's wot the Force is put 'ere for from Above. Not as 'ow we ain't fallible. We makes our mistakes. An' when we makes 'em we sticks to 'em. For the honour o' the Force. Which same is the jool Britannia wears on 'er bosom as a charm against hanarchy. That's wot the blarsted old Beaks don't understand. Yer remember Smithers of our Div?"

I remembered Smithers—well. As fine, up-standing, square-toed, bullet-headed, clean-living a son of a gun as ever perjured himself in the box. There was nothing of the softy about Smithers. I took off my billicock to Smithers' memory.

"Sacrificed to public opinion? Yuss," said Judlip, pausing at a front door and flashing his 45 c.p. down the slot of a two-grade Yale. "Sacrificed to a parcel of screamin' old women wot ort ter 'ave gorn down on their knees an' thanked Gawd for such a protector. 'E'll be out in another 'alf year. Wot'll 'e do then, pore devil? Go a bust on 'is conduc' money an' throw in 'is lot with them same hexperts wot 'ad a 'oly terror of 'im." Then Judlip swore gently.

"What should you do, O Great One, if ever it were your duty to apprehend him?"

"Do? Why, yer blessed innocent, yer don't think I'd shirk a fair clean cop? Same time, I don't say as 'ow I wouldn't 'andle 'im tender like, for sake o' wot 'e wos. Likewise 'cos 'e'd be a stiff customer to tackle. Likewise 'cos——"

He had broken off, and was peering fixedly upwards at an angle of 85° across the moonlit street. "Ullo!" he said in a hoarse whisper.

Striking an average between the direction of his eyes—for Judlip, when on the job, has a soul-stirring squint—I perceived someone in the act of emerging from a chimney-pot.

Judlip's voice clove the silence. "Wot are yer doin' hup there?"

The person addressed came to the edge of the parapet. I saw then that he had a hoary white beard, a red ulster with the hood up, and what looked like a sack over his shoulder. He said something or other in a voice like a concertina that has been left out in the rain.

"I dessay," answered my friend. "Just you come down, an' we'll see about that."

The old man nodded and smiled. Then—as I hope to be saved—he came floating gently down through the moonlight, with the sack over his shoulder and a young fir-tree clasped to his chest. He alighted in a friendly manner on the curb beside us.

Judlip was the first to recover himself. Out went his right arm, and the airman was slung round by the scruff of the neck, spilling his sack in the road. I made a bee-line for his shoulder-blades. Burglar or no burglar, he was the best airman out, and I was muchly desirous to know the precise nature of the apparatus under his ulster. A backhander from Judlip's left caused me to hop quickly aside. The prisoner was squealing and whimpering. He didn't like the feel of Judlip's knuckles at his cervical vertebræ.

"Wot wos yer doin' hup there?" asked Judlip, tightening the grip.

"I'm S-Santa Claus, Sir. P-Please, Sir, let me g-go."

"Hold him," I shouted. "He's a German."

"It's my dooty ter caution yer that wotever yer say now may be used in hevidence against yer, yer old sinner. Pick up that there sack, an' come along o' me."

The captive snivelled something about peace on earth, good will toward men.

"Yuss," said Judlip. "That's in the Noo Testament, ain't it? The Noo Testament contains some uncommon nice readin' for old gents an' young ladies. But it ain't included in the librery o' the Force. We confine ourselves to the Old Testament— O.T., 'ot. An' 'ot you'll get it. Hup with that sack, an' quick march!"

I have seen worse attempts at a neck-wrench, but it was just not slippery enough for Judlip. And the kick that Judlip then let fly was a thing of beauty and a joy for ever.

"Frog's-march him!" I shrieked, dancing. "For the love of heaven, frog's-march him!"

Trotting by Judlip's side to the Station, I reckoned it out that if Slushby had not been at the Club I should not have been here to see. Which shows that even Slushbys are put into this world for a purpose.

Bonamy Dobrée

Rudyard Kipling *

Mr. Kipling has so scrupulously winnowed the elements of his art, that his candor has deceived many into thinking him too nearly a simpleton to yield much that can be of use to them in exploring life. They are inclined to take too literally Mr. Max Beerbohm's vision of him dancing a jig with Britannia upon Hampstead Heath (after swapping hats with her), and have thought her as much belittled by his bowler as he is made ridiculous by her helmet. But it is really only the high finish of his art which makes him seem to lack subtlety, for he does not display the workings of his mind, his doubts, his gropings. He drives his thought to a conclusion; and it is only when it has reached to force of an intuition, of an assent in Newman's meaning of the word, that he clothes it in appropriate symbols.

He is, one may perhaps claim, romantic by impulse; but then he tries his romance seven times in the fire of actuality, and brings it to the clearness of crystal. Romance, for him, does not lie in yearning, but in fruition: it is not a vague beacon floating in a distant void. It may be

> A veil to draw 'twixt God his Law
> And Man's infirmity,

* [From *The Lamp and the Lute*, revised (London, 1964), pp. 38–64. First published in 1929. Reprinted by permission of Frank Cass and Co., Ltd.]

but that particular throwing up of the sponge, that sort of be-
glamouring of facts, is not permanently to his taste. What is
more to the credit of romance, in his view, is that, by imagination and faith, it brings up the 9.15. Yet if that were the end,
romance itself would be a trivial thing to make such a pother
about, even if bringing up the 9.15 does stand for building
cities and conquering continents. For even these things are
not, in themselves, of vast worth to Mr. Kipling: they are of
value only in so far as they are the mechanism which brings
action into play. For in the scheme of things as he sees it,
action is of the first and final importance, since it is action alone
which can make real for man that 'reality,' as we say, which is,
perhaps, no more than a dream in the mind of Brahma. So
small a matter as

> . . . The every day affair of business, meals and clothing
> Builds a Bulkhead 'twixt Despair and the Edge of Nothing,

for man is playing a Great Game of 'To Be, or Not to Be' in
the face of an indifferent universe, a universe as indifferent as
Hardy's. So man must work, since 'For the pain of the soul
there is, outside God's Grace, but one drug; and that is a man's
craft, learning, or other helpful motion of his own mind'; and
by the last Mr. Kipling means action, since thought by itself is
incomplete, and is only made whole through doing.

It is in the story 'The Children of the Zodiac' that Mr.
Kipling seems most wholly to express his view; and there we
read, 'You cannot pull a plough,' said the bull, with a little
touch of contempt, 'I can, and that prevents me thinking of
the Scorpion,' namely death. But that is not action as a form
of running away from thought, but rather identifying oneself
with the material of thought. There is a touch of the tragic
about Mr. Kipling. But even so the problem is not so clear
and shallow that it can be solved easily, for disillusion lurks
even behind useful action, and the void may still be there:

> As Adam was a-working outside of Eden-Wall,
> He used the Earth, he used the Seas, he used the Air and all;
> And out of black disaster
> He arose to be the master
> Of Earth and Water, Air and Fire,
> But never reached his heart's desire!
> (The Apple Tree's cut down!)

This disillusion also, it is plain, must be warded off, otherwise work (which is salvation) will not take place; and the Children of the Zodiac did not succeed in warding it off until they had learnt to laugh. Therefore Mr. Kipling also laughs, sometimes to ease his bitterness in this way, but oftener to do more than this; he laughs, not the Bergsonian laughter of social adjustment, but the impassioned, defiant laughter of Nietzsche; not the rectifying laughter of comedy, but the healing laughter of farce. Whence 'Brugglesmith,' 'The Village that Voted the Earth was Flat,' and the immortal, the Puck-like Pyecroft. Man must laugh lest he perish, just as he must work if he is to exist at all.

Yet it must not be thought that by work Mr. Kipling means fuss and hurry; he will have nothing to do with 'indecent restlessness.' As to the battle of life, that good old comforter, he remarks that 'The God who sees us all die knows that there is far too much of that battle,' and the man who created Kim's lovable lama is not blind to the possibility that his own means of defeating emptiness and evading the fear of death may be vanity. There is a rift somewhere, and Ganesh in 'The Bridge-Builders' may after all be right in regarding the toil of men but as 'dirt digging in the dirt.' There is, indeed, another possibility, and the problem is neatly put in the *Bhagavadgītā*, where Arjuna says: 'Oh Krishna, thou speakest in paradoxes, for first thou dost praise renunciation, and then praisest thou the performance of service through actions. Pray which of them has the greater merit?' It is only after some hesitation that Krishna answers, 'Verily, I say unto thee, that of the two, the performance of service is preferable to the renunciation of action.'

But there must be something behind action to justify it, and with Mr. Kipling it is a love of loyalty which reinforces his philosophy of action. First of all there is that of man to man, a loyalty born of understanding of a man's work, and the wholeness of his character. But personal loyalty, if infinitely valuable, is also horribly rare, and Mr. Kipling has no exaggerated faith in it; he has come not to hope overmuch of man. 'The raw fact of life,' Pharaoh Akhenaton told him, 'is that mankind is just a little lower than the angels, and the conventions are based on that fact in order that men may become angels. But if you begin by the convention that men are angels, they will assuredly become bigger beasts than ever.' And loyalty is an angelic quality.

This takes us a long way from the 'personal relation,' which, as we shall see, figures so large in recent literature; and, indeed, what distinguishes Mr. Kipling from so many present-day writers is precisely that he does not attempt to break down man's loneliness, seeing only futility in the balm of the 'personal relation.'

> Chase not with undesired largesse
> Of sympathy the heart
> Which, knowing her own bitterness
> Presumes to dwell apart.

That is why, when Mulvaney told him the story of 'The Courting of Dinah Shadd,' the catastrophic tale of his wooing, Mr. Kipling said nothing; he gave him a hand, which can help, but cannot heal: for at the moment when a man's black hour descends upon him, he has to fight it out alone. 'When I woke I saw Mulvaney, the night dew-gemming his moustache, leaning on his rifle at picket, lonely as Prometheus on his rock, with I know not what vultures tearing his liver.'

But since man is thus unavoidably lonely among men, there is another loyalty to serve as a spring of action, and that is a devotion to something each man must conceive of as bigger than himself. Power man has, yet

> It is not given
> For goods or gear,
> But for the Thing,

whatever the Thing may be. Mr. Kipling does not even admit the last infirmity of noble mind, for fame does not count. Thus more than sympathy, admiration, and love, go out from him to obscure men with whom 'heroism, failure, doubt, despair, and self-abnegation' are daily matters, and about whom the official reports are silent. His heart is given at once to any person who strives to do a thing well, not for praise, but through sheer love of the craftsman. For him, as for Parolles, self-love is 'the most inhibited sin in the canon'; and, after all, 'one

must always risk one's life or one's soul, or one's peace—or
some little thing.'

Here then, we see the scale of Mr. Kipling's values. First it
is essential to accept the world for what it is with no romantic
illusions, to play the man while the odds are eternally and
crushingly against you. It is hopeless to try to alter the world.
Even if you are capable of adding to it, if yours is not the ap-
pointed time your work will be sacrificed, as the medieval
priest in *Debits and Credits* had to smash his microscope, and
the Elizabethan seaman in *Rewards and Fairies* had to abandon
his idea of iron ships: the time was not yet. But man must
not complain, nor ask for life's handicap to be reduced. ' "My
right!" Ortheris answered with deep scorn. "My right! I ain't
a recruity to go whining about my rights to this and my rights
to that, just as if I couldn't look after myself. My rights! 'Strewth
A'mighty! I'm a man." ' It is that kind of individuality, that
kind of integrity, proud and secure in its own fortress, which
constitutes the aristocracy which alone is worth while, which
alone can play the Great Game of actuality.

An aristocrat is, for Mr. Kipling, one who, whatever his race
or caste or creed, has a full man within him: Ortheris, Tallantire
of the frontier district, Mahbub Ali, M'Andrew, a whole host
of them, all are aristocrats, as is Hobden the labourer, with
his sardonic smile at the changes of landlords and the unchange-
ableness of things. They are aristocrats because they care little for
themselves in comparison with what they stand for, because
they are generous, and play the Great Game with laughter on
their lips, seeking nobody's help, and claiming no reward. 'First
a man must suffer, then he must learn his work, and the self-
respect that that knowledge brings.' Never mind if he is a
failure, a tramp, or a drunkard, he may yet be an aristocrat, if
he keeps himself whole, and does not set an undue value upon
his feelings. This band of chosen naturally hates the intriguers
of Simla, or the Tomlinsons, who, when they die in their houses
in Berkeley Square, deserve neither heaven nor hell. It despises
the self-styled 'intellectuals' who 'deal with people's insides from
the point of view of men who have no stomachs.' It loathes the
rabble which whimpers, and the elements which ruin the

industrious hive, crying to the workers, 'Come here, you dear downy duck, and tell us about your feelings.' The mob which denies the loneliness of man is hateful to it, for the mob has accomplished nothing, and always defiles what it cannot understand. Thus Mr. Kipling's Utopia, unlike Mr. Wells's, is one where privacy must not be violated, and where men slink away when they find themselves part of a crowd, loathing the claims of 'the People,' who can be crueller than kings. Moreover, Mr. Kipling has only contempt for those who would marshal and pigeon-hole mankind, making it nicely tidy and neat; he feels they are ignorant of men, shallow in their analysis of motives, 'since the real reasons which make or break a man are too absurd or too obscene to be reached from the outside.' And it follows that for him 'social reform' is the selfish game of the idle.

With this aristocratic preference there goes, as so often, a sense of some Divine Ruler, for to whom else is man to dedicate his work? But Mr. Kipling has no especial choice in this direction, is no sectarian, thinking that 'when a man has come to the turnstiles of Night, all the creeds in the world seem to him wonderfully alike and colourless.' He asks of a creed only that it shall give a man the virtues he admires. 'I tell you now that the faith that takes care that every man shall keep faith, even though he may save his soul by breaking faith, is the faith for a man to believe in.' He has small opinion of Christianity because it has not eliminated the fear of the end, so that the Western world 'clings to the dread of death more closely than to the hope of life.' However, he is very tender to other people's beliefs, for men, after all, need a respite. Thus he writes of a Burmese temple, that 'Those that faced the figures prayed more zealously than the others, so I judged that their troubles were the greater.' For when all has been written and acted, his own faith also may be subject to disillusion; so with perfect consistency he may urge us 'be gentle while the heathen pray to Buddha at Kamakura.'

This, oddly enough, brings us back to Hampstead Heath, for once we speak of Mr. Kipling's religion, we speak of the British Empire. Mr. Beerbohm was cruel in his caricature, but also wittier than he appears at first sight, for he made Mr.

Kipling look a little unhappy at having thus blatantly to parade the lady of his homage. Yet one must agree that Mr. Kipling cannot be dissociated from the British Empire. It would almost seem that his mission was to bind it together in one blood-brotherhood, a purposive Masonic lodge, whose business it is to cleanse the world of shoddy. Nor can he altogether escape the suspicion of having been dazzled by it. He is enraptured by the vision of men clean of mind and thew, clear of eye and inward sight, spreading over the earth, their lands bound by the ships which fly over the sea like shuttles, weaving the clan together. His is no mere politician's picture of red on the map, since Britannia for him is a goddess. She is a goddess not only by the fact of her being, but in her nature, for she exacts much toil from her votaries, much of the silent endurance, abnegation, and loyalty that he loves. The Empire then is to be cherished, not so much because it is in itself an achievement, but because, like old Rome, it is the most superb instrument to cause man to out-face the universe, assert himself against vacancy. Since it unifies the impulses needed to do this, it is Mr. Kipling's Catholic Church.

These things being, apparently, the basis of Mr. Kipling's thought (though the Empire is, strictly speaking, only an accident, an expression rather than a necessity), we may now ask ourselves, honestly facing the risk of being impudent and unduly probing, of what impulses this thought is the satisfaction. And at the foundation of his philosophic love of action we are tempted to find that pining for action men often have, when, for one reason or another, it is denied them. He sometimes comes near to blaspheming against his art, echoing James Thomson's

> Singing is sweet, but be sure of this;
> Lips only sing when they cannot kiss,

as though the mere act of writing were itself proof of impotence or frustration. This is not a final attitude, but it indicates what may lie behind Mr. Kipling's adoration of perfectly insufferable and not altogether real subalterns, and others, who in various degrees (so long as it is not from offices) handle the affairs of the world.

Yet, ultimately, he is too good a craftsman, too whole an artist, not to see that God, or whatever other name he may be known by, is to be praised in more ways than the obvious. Nevertheless, he now and again reaches out for support to the knowledge that he also is playing the great game, if not of the universe, at least of the world, and is as worthy of a number as Kim, Mahbub Ali, or Hurree Babu:

> Who once hath dealt in the widest game
> > That all of a man can play,
> No later love, no larger fame
> > Will lure him long away.
> As the war-horse smelleth the battle afar,
> > The entered Soul, no, less
> He saith 'Ha! Ha!' where the trumpets are
> And the thunders of the Press.

Such an attitude permanently held would be far too jejune to produce the real intensity of vision we get from Mr. Kipling; and luckily for us, he has at bottom that worship of his own craft he so much admires in others. Addressing his God, his subtilized Jehovah, who judges man by his deeds, he says:

> Who lest all thought of Eden fade
> > Bring'st Eden to the craftsman's brain,
> God-like to muse on his own trade,
> > And Man-like stand with God again.

There he is the priest of the Mysterious Will, who causes all things to come in their due time; but one feels he still sometimes needs to justify his work to himself. He is urged to make it plain that all his stories are parables. Thus:

> When all the world would have a matter hid,
> > Since truth is seldom friend to any crowd
> Men write in fable, as old Æsop did,
> > Jesting at that which none will name aloud.
> And this they needs must do, or it will fall
> > Unless they please, they are not heard at all.

It is clear that for Mr. Kipling, art is not an escape: it is a precision of bare facts, which his art must make palatable.

Further, since the choice of a goddess does not lie altogether within a man's mental scope, we may seek in Mr. Kipling's impulses the reason for his profound satisfaction in the Empire.

and his need to assert it. Perhaps the most important of these is his craving to belong to something, a love, not of 'the little platoon,' to use Burke's phrase, but of the large regiment. 'It must be pleasant to have a country of one's own to show off,' he remarks. Indeed, his craving for roots makes even the deck of a P. and O. British soil; British, not English, because he is a citizen of the Empire, not of England alone: for if it were essential to be the latter, he would be partly dispossessed. Having spent so many of his early years in India, he is not wholly of England: indeed, India is the place where he really belongs. When, for instance, in 1913, he visited Cairo, he wrote: 'It is true that the call to prayer, the cadence of some of the street cries, and the cut of some of the garments differed a little from what I had been brought up to; but for the rest, the shadow on the dial had turned back twenty degrees for me, and I found myself saying, as perhaps the dead say when they have recovered their wits, "This is my real world again!" ' But he is not an Indian, he is an Englishman; therefore, to be an integral whole, he must at all costs make England and the Empire one.

His love of the Empire, and his admiration for those virtues it brings out in men, make him apt to find qualities in Englishmen only which really exist in all races; and this is part of the deformation Mr. Kipling the artist has at times undergone at the hands of Mr. Kipling the man of action, who found his weapon in the press, and his altar in the Empire. If there had been no daily, or weekly, or monthly papers, he might have remained a priest; but in his middle days he fell into the encouraging hands of W. E. Henley, then, in 1893, editing *The National Observer*. Though this gave his talent scope, it meant that instead of speaking only to those who would understand his very special philosophy, he began to proselytize, and shout too loud into the deaf ears of Demos. His work suffered by the accidents of time and circumstance, by the mischance that he was born into an age of magazines and newspapers, when the listeners are the many, and not the aristocrats to whom he naturally belongs. It took him, with his slightly unhappy expression, on to Hampstead Heath. A change came over his work, and the echo of the voice of Henley 'throwing a chest' (another man of action to whom action was denied) is every now and again heard between the lines. In 1893 he published *Many Inventions*, a rich, varied, and mature work which might be singled out as the best volume of his stories, unless *Life's Handicap* be preferred; but from that year, when he joined Henley, his writing took on a more obviously didactic hue, and we have *The Day's Work*, such parables as 'A Walking Delegate,' that tale of perfectly dutiful horses kicking the Trades-Union-Agitator horse. In 1887, or thereabouts, he was writing his delightful *Letters of Marque*, with their profound tolerance of India: in 1907 he wrote for *The Morning Post* the clangorous *Letters to the Family*. The man who had in earlier years remarked 'He began to understand why Boondi does not encourage Englishman,' could later complain 'Yet South Africa could even now be made a tourists' place—if only the railroad and the steamship lines had faith.' That is shocking. It is true that he had always loved the Empire, but not in the Hampstead Heath way; and surely it was the exigencies of this later didactic journalism which turned him from a priest into an advance booking agent, and forced him into too extravagant a statement of 'British' qualities. He does not, however, in all his work assume that these are the monopoly of the British, for he awards his due to the Frenchman and the Sikh, and even to the Bengali, when he really gives rein to his profound instincts, and forgets the thunders of the press. Therefore the distortion does not matter in the long run, for time and again he gives us things of a breadth and a peculiar grip we get from no other writer of his generation.

The accidents, then, of Mr. Kipling's attitude may be dismissed, to allow us to return to his intuitions, and proceed to the next step in our analysis, namely, a consideration of what symbols he has chosen to clothe his intuitions in. He has usually chosen men and women to body forth his notions—his plots have no great symbolic importance; and thus his people, as is always the case in really creative art, represent something beyond themselves. They are not merely vehicles for an idle tale. Where he has chosen other material, as in 'The Mother Hive,' or 'The Ship that Found Herself,' he has failed, as any one is bound to do. An apologue always smacks of the schoolroom, and it is worth noticing that these stories belong to his most didactic period. He is not quite at his ease there, his assent is a little forced; but when his intuition was whole, as in *Kim*, in which the artist conquers the moralist and buries him deep under ground, he is nothing short of superb: his symbols clothe his intuition so that we take it for flesh and blood. That is, we work from life to the thought, and not from the thought to life, as we do with lesser artists, who have ideas they wish to impose upon life. Mr. Kipling's failures occur either when his shallower, demagogue nature takes charge, and we are conscious of didacticism; or where the intuition is uncompleted. It is uncompleted in two sets of instances: the first where women are concerned, whence Mrs. Hauksbee, Mrs. Gadsby, and others, where the symbols are vulgar because the intuition is false (there is a reservation to be made in the case of the woman in the last story in *Debits and Credits*); the second is in the mysterious world of unreality which he feels about him, but which he has not resolved within himself: hence such failures—one must here defy popular opinion—as 'They,' and 'The Brushwood Boy.' There the symbols are sentimental, not because the intuition is feeble, but because it has not been resolved into art.

So far an attempt has been made to define Mr. Kipling's philosophic apparatus; but without delight, and perhaps an attitude of praise, there can be no great art after his manner, and these he has abundantly. A *Diversity of Creatures*; that is not only the title of a book, it is a phrase which occurs often in other of his volumes, and he often thanks God for the variety of His beings. He is an apt illustration for those who claim that only by adoring what is can one add to life; and *quia multum amavit* is a passport to his heaven. He revels in men so long as they are positive, since it is only by his deeds that man can exist. Also, with a generous sensuality which rejects no physical sensation, he loves 'the good brown earth,' especially the smells that it produces, West or East. With all these likes, with his keen senses, his recognition of adventure in life and his feeling for romance in works, and his zestful following of men on their occasions lawful and unlawful, he has God's plenty within him.

Thus it is that his best symbols also have God's plenty within them. It is noticeable that they are not like those of Tchekov, say, or of Henry James, since different symbols correspond with different intuitions, and his are not theirs. There is nothing rarefied about them. Mr. Kipling's live close to the ground, and he has frequented the more primitive sort of men because 'all the earth is full of tales to him who listens and does not drive the poor away from his door. The poor are the best of tale-tellers, for they must lay their ear to the ground every night.' He met a hundred men on the road to Delhi, and they were all his brothers, since they lived close to the actualities that can be handled. They were the people in *Kim*, there were Peachey Carnehan and Daniel Dravot (in 'The Man who would be King'); there were forgotten toilers in out-stations, and above all there were Mulvaney, Ortheris, and Learoyd. Nor must it pass unnoticed that all his three soldiers had trodden paths of bitterness ('first a man must suffer'), and were at times subject to an overwhelming sorrow akin to madness, the sorrow of disillusion. They are of value as symbols precisely because they have outfaced much. They were none of them obviously successful, for Mr. Kipling despises success except that which consists in keeping one's soul intact. Whence his sympathy for those who are broken because they are too positive, such as the sometime Fellow of an Oxford college who had passed 'outside the pale,' for the lighthouse man who went mad because of the infernal streakiness of the tides, and even for Love o' Women. In such cases, where human beings seem wholly to live the life of the symbol and to exist as a quality, Mr. Kipling is content that men should be no more than a part of the earth; he is happy to be their interpreter, and give them their place as players of the Great Game.

If, at this point, we try to mark what it is that most distinguishes Mr. Kipling from other writers of our period, we find that he shares with most the despondency of the day, but not its optimism as regards panceas such as support Mr. Wells and Mr. Shaw; and that his delight in the actuality of men, in their proven virtues, gives him values instead of vague hopes. In his metaphysical scepticism, in his belief in the void which surrounds existence he is a child of his time, as modern as any of our literary nihilists who see, in Mr. Housman's phrase, that 'when men think they fasten their hands upon their

hearts.' Indeed, it is safe to say that at no modern period has
the world seemed so empty a thing, the universe so indifferent,
our values so factitious; and as we look back upon the centuries
we can see that this attitude has been fatefully coming upon
us. Yet, though Mr. Kipling manifests this attitude, he differs
from his contemporaries, and it is because of this difference that
he already seems to survive them. He is more enduring, because something of the past three centuries clings to him.

For the Elizabethans and Jacobeans, life gained its glamour
largely from its nearness to the plague-pit; its values were determined and heightened by the vigorously expressed dogmas of
a church which, for pulpit reasons at least, believed in Hell;
the metaphysical void was filled with a sense that life was given
man as a discipline and an adventure: this is still part of Mr.
Kipling's belief. Indeed, if one were to have to choose one man
from whom he descends rather than another, one would light
upon Jeremy Taylor. In *Holy Dying* we read:

> Softness is for slaves and beasts, for minstrels and useless persons,
> for such as cannot ascend higher than the state of a fair ox, or a
> servant entertained for vainer offices: but the man that designs his
> son for noble employments, to honours and to triumphs, to consular
> dignities and presidencies of councils, loves to see him pale with
> study, or panting with labour, hardened with sufferance, or eminent
> by dangers. And so God dresses us for heaven.

And in *Letters of Travel* Mr. Kipling writes:

> I wonder sometimes whether any eminent novelist, philosopher,
> dramatist, or divine of to-day, has to exercise half the pure imagina-
> tion, not to mention insight, endurance, and self-restraint, which is
> accepted without comment in what is called 'the material exploita-
> tion' of a new country. Take only the question of creating a new
> city at the juncture of two lines—all three in the air. The mere
> drama of it, the play of human virtues, would fill a book. And when
> the work is finished, when the city is, when the new lines embrace
> a new belt of farms, and the tide of wheat has rolled North another
> unexpected degree, the men who did it break off, without compli-
> ments, to repeat the joke elsewhere.

The mind is the same; the matter only the difference of the
centuries.

Then, with the advance of science and the retreat of the
plague, man grew less concerned with himself and heaven, and

more interested in the outer world, its marvels, its emerging order. Coupled with a somewhat flabby Deism, believing at the most in only a luke-warm Hell, was the attitude of mind typified by John Evelyn, who, like Mr. Kipling, found naught common on the earth. Here Mr. Kipling largely stays, and with the introspective movement which found its prophet in Rousseau, with the hysterical subjective idealists whose only reality is their emotion, he will have nothing to do, and it is likely that Proust seems a dreary waste to him. He cannot away with men and women intent upon saving their souls, or who believe even, that they have souls worth the saving. It is typical that he should describe a man he dislikes as 'fearing physical pain as some men fear sin.'

Yet the solipsist attitude still further weakened the idea of future punishment, and we are not surprised that in the century and a half which saw its development, an English Lord Chancellor, Lord Westbury, should, in a famous judgment, have 'dismissed Hell with costs, and taken away from orthodox members of the Church of England their last hope of everlasting damnation.' This was to have its effect; but habits of impulse are slow to change, and if there was to be no Hell, there was still to be service to God; and of this sense again Mr. Kipling retains something, since, as far as meaning goes, it might have been not he, but Browning who wrote:

> One instant's toil to Thee denied
> Stands all eternity's offence.

But soon it came to be seen that if there was no Hell, the only Heaven would have to be on earth; and if social reform began at least as early as Shaftesbury, not to go back to Shelburne, it is chiefly characteristic of the Edwardian period. Mr. Kipling, however, who cannot bear the flaccidity of social reform, its interference of people with each other, still has a hope of Hell; and agreeing that this world suffices for man, places his Hell upon earth. Thus he cannot accept our modern Utopias, so neat and hygienic, so free from temptation and sin and suffering— except, for him, the suffering of being in a crowd. Utopian perfection would be loathsomely insipid, and we may surmise that the final reason why the British Empire satisfies him, is that it can contain both Heaven and Hell, at least as much as is good for any man.

Apart from the delight which he gives, an important reservation, it is doubtful if the real value of any writer is apparent to his close contemporaries: his equals in age are likely to seize upon those things they already share with him, rather than greet what is original; and, with mankind's aversion for what is new in ideas, reject what the next generation will eagerly clutch at. As far as can be judged at present, the elements in Mr. Kipling's work which have won him popularity are the least important, the most ephemeral. It will only be possible to give him his rightful place when the political heats of his day have become coldly historical. But to us, the successive generation, he has a value that may well be permanent, apart from his language, which itself deserves to live. He has indicated an attitude towards life which, to us groping for a solid basis, may serve, if not for that basis itself, then as a point of disagreement. He deals, after all, with the enduring problems of humanity, the problems out of which all religion, all real poetry must arise. Moreover, he provides a solution which those of his own cast of mind—and they are many, though most may be unaware of it—will greet with satisfaction, and even with that sense of glamour, of invigoration, which it is partly the function of good literature to give.

II   THE BREAKING STRAIN, HEALING AND COMPASSION

The more one reads Kipling, the more complex and baffling he becomes: and here I would like to bring forward a highly individual, recurring, and important element in his make-up which has hardly been noticed. It is, perhaps, very relevant to our present-day atmosphere of strain, our *angst* if you like to call it so. A great deal has been written about him in the last twenty years, not only here but in France, Italy, and latterly in America, mainly about his prose; but since this aspect has been missed, something always nags at my mind telling me: 'No; that isn't quite what he meant. It isn't there exactly that he matters.'

Something more, it is true, has been done about his poetry, notably by Mr. T. S. Eliot in his enormously valuable study;

but what he actually chose for his anthology is, if only by accident, a trifle tendentious, because he was making out the case for Kipling as a superb ballad and hymn writer. He was far more than that, far subtler and more sensitive, as hinted, but not much more than hinted, by Mr. T. R. Henn in *The Apple and the Spectroscope*. Many of the poems, moreover, are complementary to the stories, poem and story making a complete whole. But, taken all in all, in nearly everything written about him the discussion is still too much overshadowed by politics (the process of shedding this aspect is taking longer than I hoped earlier), as, for example, in Mr. Edmund Wilson's *The Wound and the Bow*. Surely now that the tumult and the shouting have died, it ought to be possible to see Kipling objectively: he is no longer part of the political picture.

It is not to be denied that one has to look at his imperialism. But it was not chauvinistic, as most people used to think— and some still do—since he always upbraided the jingo. Actually, his conception of the Empire was in the tradition of the great myth of beneficent world-government which stirred Shakespeare when he wrote the final speech of Cranmer in *Henry VIII*, which comes out in D'avenant, and still more grandly in Dryden's *Annus Mirabilis* and Pope's *Windsor Forest*. It was a poetic idea. Further, the Empire was important for Kipling, because, as explained in my earlier essay, it was something a man could devote himself to, an object of the kind of faith Kipling was always looking for. Having seen men broken, in soul as well as in body, through selflessly carrying out the daily work of the Empire, unthanked, unrewarded, even reviled, he gave the Empire his *conditional* allegiance.

And then, because he accepted, especially in his early days, the fact that men did horrible things to each other, he could not be a philosophic 'optimist,' *à la* Shaftesbury, but was, rather, a 'pessimist' in the line of Swift. He could not help, therefore, rejecting the idea of man as a benevolent creature, and in so doing he trod on a good many 'advanced' toes. As a result he is continually being accused of illiberalism, as, for instance, by Professor Lionel Trilling in his fine book *The Liberal Imagination*. How far Kipling may have been right in that respect, as against his critics, the history of the world in the last fifty years may help us to judge.

It is not, however, the purpose here to defend Kipling on that sort of issue; it is, rather, to penetrate a region which nobody seems to have explored,[1] into something which more than offsets that apparently callous, almost cruel element in him which outrages a good many people, and made Harold Laski say that Kipling 'will symbolize the literature of hate, of malignant grandiosity.' This attitude persists; we get, for instance, Professor V. de S. Pinto in his *Crisis in English Poetry* regarding him as the apostle of brute force. Nothing can be further from the truth. He symbolizes not hate, but a deep compassion; not malignant grandiosity and brute force, but humility, and tenderness amounting to deep pity. Re-reading him, especially his later work, one cannot but be impressed by this note of his, repeatedly and emphatically struck; and, more significant still, by his intense interest about, one might say his deep feeling for, healing, and the means of healing.

First, however, must be noted a curious thread which runs through all his work, which can be described only as his "descents into hell,' not only into those places where the soul is lonely and has to face itself, but into the overwhelming hells that blot out. Take this description:

. . . Just then . . . I was aware of a little grey shadow, as it might have been a snowflake seen against the light, floating at an immense distance in the background of my brain. It annoyed me, and I shook my head to get rid of it. Then my brain telegraphed that is was the fore-runner of a swift-striding gloom. . . . The gloom overtook me . . . and my amazed and angry soul dropped, gulf by gulf, into that horror of great darkness which is spoken of in the Bible.

That passage, outrageously cut, is from 'The House Surgeon,' a story in *Actions and Reactions*, and it is followed by a poem, which, if pondered, is horrifying, but which some have found insensitive, perhaps because it is written in the direct language and simple rhythm of hymns:

> If thought can reach to Heaven
> On Heaven let it dwell,
> For fear that Thought be given
> Like power to reach to Hell.

1 This was written before the appearance of the admirable *The Art of Rudyard Kipling*, by J. M. S. Tompkins.

—lines which are revealing enough. Similarly, a typical periodical descent into the abyss overtakes the two people of the story 'In the Same Boat,' to be found in A *Diversity of Creatures*, as early as 1917. And in his last two books Kipling again and again returns to the theme of the great darkness.

He had touched on the same sort of thing in his earlier stories. There is, for instance, 'At the End of the Passage' in *Life's Handicap*, which came out in 1891, in which the desperately overworked Indian civilian dies because, as his servant commented, he had descended into the Dark Places. From the beginning, then, Kipling had been drawn to tales of mental breakdown, of suffering made unbearable from one cause or another: that, say, of the lighthouse keeper who went mad from loneliness, or the reproved subaltern who shot himself in despair. There are dozens of them. But a change came over his treatment of the theme. In his younger days he was eager only to tell the stories as part of the enthralling, darkly striated pageant of life; later he became interested in the causes, and finally he was absorbed in the healing of the horror, the point to be expanded here. Obviously he knew all about the horror; as he said after the extract quoted, the state 'has to be experienced to be appreciated,' and you do not have to read far to know how agonisingly he had himself experienced it. Perhaps that is why to some people he seems so callous about physical pain; he certainly despised people who feared it, knowing that it was nothing compared with spirtual agony. This he stated unequivocally in the 'Hymn to Physical Pain,' of which the first and last stanzas run:

> Dread Mother of Forgetfulness
> Who, when Thy reign begins,
> Wipest away the Soul's distress,
> And memory of her sins. . . .

> Wherefore we praise Thee in the deep,
> And on our beds we pray
> For Thy return that Thou may'st keep
> The Pains of Hell at bay!

It is clear that Kipling, who suffered a good deal of physical pain in his later life, was at intervals catastrophically disturbed.

Looking at the stories concerned with these states, you see
that they all come about from too much strain on people. The
sense of this probably lay far back in Kipling's experience, when,
as a small boy living in the house at Southsea while his parents
were in India, he underwent the purgatory he was to describe
in the terrible story 'Baa, Baa, Black Sheep.' But the early
tales which have as their climax a breakdown from strain do
not on the whole take the matter any further; in the later
stories, however, Kipling became, significantly, interested not
so much in the states of horror themselves, as in their cure; the
cure, if you like, of neuroses which are the effects of strain,
usually caused by devotion to duty (often in the war), but sometimes through the operation of sheer fate. Together with this,
Kipling grew to be ever more deeply interested in the amount
of strain a human being could stand without breaking down.
Partly to resolve this, he evolved those strange stories which
pictured what he called 'The Order Above' (which, by a sort of
inverted Platonism, he regarded as a reflection of 'The Order
Below'), symbolized by the Archangels, Satan, and other
heavenly principalities and powers. In the last of these tales,
'Uncovenanted Mercies,' the souls of men and women are 're-
conditioned' for service as guardian angels, the final point of
the process being, as Satan puts it, 'a full test for Ultimate
Breaking Strain.' The technical phrase struck Kipling, and the
year before his death he published the 'Hymn of Breaking
Strain,' the load to which men are ruthlessly subjected. A por-
tion of it reads:

> The careful text-books measure
> (Let all who build beware!)
> The load, the shock, the pressure
> Material can bear. . . .
>
> But, in our daily dealing
> With stone and steel, we find
> The Gods have no such feeling
> Of justice toward mankind.
> To no set gauge they make us,—
> For no laid course prepare—
> And presently o'ertake us
> With loads we cannot bear:
> *Too merciless to bear.*

But Kipling will not encourage whining. The poem tells us at the end, that if man serves 'the veiled and secret Power, in spite of being broken, because of being broken,' he can stand up and build anew.

If, then, the world includes hells for men and women so intolerable that the strain actually breaks them, what is the cure? Kipling had all sorts of mechanisms for healing, varieties of psycho-analysis which clear up complexes. But these are merely mechanisms, and the driving force, the virtue without which no cure can be effective, is—and this can be boldly stated—compassion. He realized very early, as an intuition, with what Newman would have called 'complete assent,' that man is fated to suffer and to be lonely; that when a man's black hour descends upon him he has to fight it out alone, indeed would rather fight it out alone, as did Mulvaney—himself, incidentally, a healer. When in *Debits and Credits* he said that 'for the pain of the soul there is, outside God's grace, but one drug . . .' stress must be placed on God's grace, which is compassion. One becomes, perhaps startlingly, aware of this from the story 'The Gardener' in the same volume. This is concerned with a woman whose adored natural son—whom she passes off as her nephew—is killed in the war. She goes to the war cemetery to visit his grave, and finds there a man firming in the young plants, who asks, 'What are you looking for?' She gives the name and adds: 'My nephew.' The story ends:

The man lifted his eyes and looked at her with infinite compassion before he turned from the fresh-sown grass toward the naked black crosses.

'Come with me,' he said, 'and I will show you where your son lies.'

When Helen left the cemetery she turned for a last look. In the distance she saw the man bending over his young plants; and she went away, supposing him to be the gardener.

Though Kipling may not have been in any ordinary sense of the word a Christian, it would seem clear that this Gospel reference to Mary Magdalene meeting Christ at the Tomb is profoundly revealing of his attitude. If this were an isolated case, it would not perhaps count for much: but the attitude is evident again and again, as in 'Uncovenanted Mercies,' already touched upon. After Satan's remark about the Ultimate

Breaking Strain the story goes on: ' "But now?" Gabriel demanded. "Why do you ask?" "Because it was written *Even Evil
itself shall pity.*" ' It may be noted too that the choruses of the
poem which concludes the similar story 'On the Gate' in *Debits
and Credits* consist, certainly, of Glories, Powers, and Toils, but
also—and this one ought to notice—of Patiences, Faiths, Hopes,
and Loves.

This point could be illustrated over and over; but now attention may be drawn to the remarkable series of stories which
treat of healing, especially those in the later volumes, 'the Kipling that nobody reads,' as G. M. Young put it in his article
in *The Dictionary of National Biography*. Kipling was perpetually interested in doctors and doctoring, and was much the
friend of the famous Sir John Bland Sutton, who figures as
Sir James Belton in the story 'The Tender Achilles' in Kipling's
last collection. Time and again he demands of medical research
less thinking and more imagination; let us have bolder speculation, he begged the doctors, rather than improved technique.
He himself had amazing, not to say visionary, notions about
healing. He touched on them first, to any degree, in 'A Doctor
of Medicine'—*Rewards and Fairies*—where the seventeenth-
century astrologer-physician, Nicolas Culpeper, utters very
strange doctrine. Kipling dared develop such notions in an
after-dinner speech made to the Royal Society of Medicine in
1928, when he made a plea for doctoring to return—on a
modern basis—to the astrological idea of 'influences.' He argued
that: 'Nicolas Culpeper, were he with us now, would find that
the essential unity of creation is admitted in so far forth as we
have plumbed infinity; and that man, Culpeper's epitome of all,
is in himself a universe of universes, each universe ordered—
negatively and positively—by sympathy and antipathy— on the
same lines as hold the stars in their courses.' Soon he put some
of these ideas into the story 'Unprofessional,' where the medical
men study what seem to be tides in malignant tissues. They
discuss radium, as astrologers might discuss planetary influences,
the analogy Kipling had made use of in his speech to the Royal
Society of Medicine. No doubt he knew that all this was the
wildest speculation—yet, was it so daft? One of the people in
the story says: 'It's crazy mad,' but another reports, 'Which was
what the Admiralty said at first about steam in the Navy.'

Some of the tales, as already noted, are on a more psycho-analytical level, and at least two of his cases of war neurosis are cured by what might be called Freudian therapeutics.

Yet healing, that urgent business, might be brought about by other means—even by laughter, which for Kipling, as for Meredith, was always one of the great healers. Another story from his last book, 'The Miracle of St. Jubanus,' will serve to illustrate this. The centre of the tale is a village priest, drawn with extraordinary tenderness and understanding. One of his parishioners is a returned peasant-soldier suffering from what we used to call, a little euphemistically, shell-shock. He was one of those who, in the priest's words, 'entered hells of whose existence they had not dreamed—of whose terrors they lacked words to tell.' He would 'hide himself for an hour or two, and come back visibly replunged in his torments.' Being made to laugh restored him from near-idiocy to normality. Kipling, then, sought every way of cure; he was passionately concerned to relieve the sufferings of humanity which, in the last resort, can end only in death. Time and again one finds in him an immense pity, especially for those who, as he liked to put it, had fought with the beasts at Ephesus, beasts far more terrible than the actual beasts of the Epistle of St. Paul. Though not, to repeat, so far as one can judge, a Christian, one could perhaps say that he adhered to the perennial philosophy and verged on mysticism; certainly he shared with the Hindus their tolerance of all attempts to bear the burden of the mystery:

> O ye who tread the Narrow Way
> By Tophet-flare to Judgment Day,
> Be gentle when 'the heathen' pray
> To Buddha at Kamakura!

It did not matter to him where a man got his beliefs, so long as his religion could tell him what is said in II. *Samuel* xxv.14: 'Yet God doth devise that his banished be not expelled from him.' Surely those are not the words of a man who symbolizes the literature of hate and malignity, but of one who, for all his rough scorns, and his sometimes infuriating blindness to the other side of the question, symbolizes, rather, a profound, understanding compassion.

Boris Ford

A Case For Kipling? *

> . . . talked pure Brasenose to him for
> three minutes. Otherwise he spoke and
> wrote trade-English—a toothsome amal-
> gam of Americanisms and epigram.—
> "THE VILLAGE THAT VOTED THE EARTH
> WAS FLAT."

MR. ELIOT'S CRITICISM, at the period when it was evidently a
product of the same mind and interests as also created the poetry, was not only bodied in some of the most aristocratic prose
of the century, but displayed an intelligence that gave his judgments a rare authority and confidence. Not, one must admit,
that Mr. Eliot was ever a wholly reliable critic, and often one
was compelled to modify or even disagree with particular valua-
tions. But throughout the early work the direction of argument
was evident, tending to the refashioning of obliterated standards, and above all to a conception of art and literature as the
product of a lively interplay of individual integrity and social
vigour.

In the course of the introductory essay to his choice of poems
by Kipling, Mr. Eliot writes: "Having previously exhibited an
imaginative grasp of space, and England in it, he now proceeds
to a similar achievement in time"; and he quotes in support of
this shift of activity the following tales: "An Habitation Enforced," "My Son's Wife," and "The Wish House." Now, what
is striking about this particular judgment is not that it is so indefinite as to be hardly worth making, for it shares this blemish
with the rest of the essay, but that Mr. Eliot should now practice
a critical discipline that permits him to reproduce verbatim

---

* [From *The Importance of Scrutiny*, ed. Eric Bentley (New York,
1948), pp. 324–337. First published in *Scrutiny*, XI, No. 1 (1942). Reprinted by permission of the author.]

and without acknowledgement (that is, unconsciously) the indefinite judgments of others. For in his book on Kipling, Mr. Shanks writes: "England now gave him not merely consolation but a new extension of life. Whereas on his departure from India he had sought this extension in space, he now found it in time"; and he in turn quotes the following stories: "An Habitation Enforced," "Friendly Brook," "The Wish House," and "My Son's Wife." But one should not deduce from this that Mr. Eliot's essay is nothing but plagiarism of lesser critics, for much of it is a stylistic plagiarism of Mr. Eliot himself. There is the familiar air of subtle differentiation, coupled with the pervasive refusal to observe any precise demarcations. The tone has about it that judicious detachment which was once so suggestive of meaning but is now employed simply to disarm criticism and to enforce a personal view. Indeed, Mr. Eliot seems to feel himself in a new role, that of legal panjandrum, when he admits that readers unacquainted with Kipling "might perhaps imagine that I had been briefed in the cause of some hopelessly second-rate writer, and that I was trying, as an exhibition of my ingenuity as an advocate, to secure some small remission of the penalty of oblivion." And though Kipling, anxious to stand well with posterity, expressed some anxiety as to who, "when our story comes to be told, will have the telling of it," one feels that he would have hesitated before inviting the author of *Triumphal March* to undertake the task. In fact, Mr. Eliot has all too evidently briefed himself. And at least one of the clues to the enigma has already been suggested; whereas Mr. Eliot's best criticism related to his poetic interests, his critical concern for Kipling is accompanied by the admission that "part of the fascination of this subject is the exploration of a mind so different from my own." In fact, if the two minds are still (or so one hopes) poetically exclusive, as individuals one can detect a certain affiliation, or in the case of Mr. Eliot a would-be affiliation, between the men; unfortunately, it is the human rather than the artistic factor that seems to have predominated.

The main case against the claim that Kipling revealed an imaginative grasp on space and then on time is that the imagination he revealed in the process has far more in common with that of the industrial pioneer, the man who exploits the backward area, than with that of the artist, who by contrast opens up inner regions of individual feeling. By this I do not mean here to imply the usual criticism of Kipling, that he was the voice of British imperialism, but rather and more relevantly that his mind was a very crude instrument, seldom if ever in touch with finer spiritual issues, and that in consequence his grasp on anything at all delicate has about it the virtuosity of the Chinese juggler. He found, very early on in his career, that he possessed a facility for conveying the atmosphere of a people and the type-emotions of an individual, and he spent a lifetime exploiting and developing this talent. But essentially the process is that of the news-camera, of the highly efficient journalist eye, and the journalist ear and nose and palate as well. It is on this level, and not, for instance, as implying a concern analogous to Hopkins's struggle with language, that one has to understand Kipling's remark that "it is necessary that every word should tell, carry, weigh, taste and, if need be, smell." And exactly what this means in practice can be seen in *Kim*, which Mr. Eliot in fact quotes in this context and which he feels to be Kipling's "greatest book." This novel is so disarmingly superficial that even its less pleasant elements, those relating to the colour conflict, fail to give any sharp offence. And if indeed it seems to be one of his most satisfactory works, that is because the author's main interest is still (the book appeared in 1901) that of the boggle-eyed and fascinated initiate, and not yet that of the legislator. As he himself wrote: "*Kim*, of course, was nakedly picaresque and plotless—a thing imposed from without." However, most often his flights of imagination, whether in space or time, seem to me merely ineffectual. Mr. Eliot quotes at length, and with admiration, from "The Finest Story in the World"; and certainly it is a test-case, since here Kipling faces himself not only with the ordinary job of writing an efficient tale, but with the added task of hinting at the "finest story in the world," and of convincing his reader that it is as fine as the tale demands. Actually this "finest story" seems to consist of nothing but a set of historical-cameos of a fairly vivid and entirely trivial nature, and these distinct episodes are related to each other not with a view to illustrating historical continuity, but simply as a means to dramatizing a crude belief in metempsychosis. The quality of imagination displayed is that of the scenario-writer, and the tale as a whole is on the level of *The Strand Magazine*. For all Mr. Eliot's remark that Kipling "is almost 'possessed' of a kind of second-sight," his vision, whether of the normal or the psychic variety, remains consistently that of the journalist, and his reconstructions of the past have as little *artistic* interest as his descriptions of the present. Except for children, there seems little to be said on behalf of this imagination; but of course, though children probably do enjoy *Puck of Pook's Hill* and the *Jungle Books*, Kipling rather hoped that adults would like them too, and hence the claims, often made on their behalf by his admirers, that they reveal a mature and subtle sense of historical tradition. Mr. Eliot, before supporting such an idea, might profitably read through some of his own essays dealing with tradition and continuity.

That Kipling is essentially a journalist, almost the founder of modern journalism, seems generally admitted; and for most people his name is also associated with a reverence for the machine of British imperialism. In any ordinary sense of the terms, these charges cannot profitably be denied; though Mr. Eliot devotes a full page of equivocations to the matter, even to answering the accusation that Kipling was a fascist (which surely no one with a sense for chronological exactitude can have made) with the retort that fascism "from the truly Tory point of view is merely the extreme degradation of democracy"; and concluding, in reply to the suggestion that Kipling believed in racial superiority, by quoting his genuine sympathy for the Indians in *Kim*, despite the fact that the whole point of that book, or at least its climax, is Kim's assertion of superiority, at the moment of crisis, simply by virtue of his white parentage, and his subsequent willingness to use his Hindu affiliations in the service of the white foreigners. After one has said all that can be said for Kipling, as Mr. George Orwell has said it (see *Dickens, Dali and Others*), after one has admitted his historical value, or his verbal dexterity, or has commended him as a "great verse-writer" or as a "good bad poet," or has stressed his undoubted sense of national responsibility—after saying all this and a great deal else, one inevitably returns to what seem to me the two fundamental issues: that Kipling developed in the

1890's, and that he suffered the common disability of an artistic decadence, which is an atrophy of finer feeling. Ultimately all one's criticisms resolve themselves to this historical considera- tion, on the one hand, and to the moral issue, on the other. And because the case has been made repeatedly on the level of the particular, I wish here simply to consider the implications of these more general issues.

Perhaps the main feature of the last decade of the nineteenth century in this country was its internal irruption. One thinks too exclusively of the 1890's as the era of Dandyism and the Decadence, of Wilde and Beardsley, forgetting that it was also a period both of imperial expansion and of the new socialism, of Rhodes and of the Webbs. It was, in fact, a period of social disintegration. The gaudy triumphs of imperialism, culminating in Mafeking Night, fostered, in the energy released, a spirit of irresponsibility in the realm of ideas. The key-word of the decade was *new*, and this concern expressed itself in two main ways: in literature, and in art generally, the new was expressed in a cult of virtuosity, a search for the exotic and the rare, and in a taste for antithesis and epigram; while in the social and political sphere, it showed itself in a flowering of socialist and Fabian ideas, on the one hand, and, on the other, in a realization by imperialism of its unsuspected power and dominion. At a somewhat analogous period, Marlowe gives expression to a similar combination of circumstances, and if his liking for sonorous and exotic language and his idealization of the mer- chant-adventurer were not inimical to the production of fine art, that was due to a set of cultural circumstances, above all perhaps to a social homogeneity, that was no longer operative when Kipling came to the fore. The impoverishment of life left his work as shallow as Marlowe's had been vigorous, and the atomization of the social scene found him hovering be- tween the superficially divergent worlds of art and politics, much as Wilde also toyed with socialism and Wells with literature.

Kipling's early life in India gave him, almost inevitably, the imperial outlook and the colour prejudice. But he was also born of artistic parents, and became a close friend of Burne-Jones. And thus he came to satisfy his longings for a life of active service to the Empire, a life he was never able to experience except by proxy, through the medium of his writing. The consequences of such a combination are not sympathetic. The Empire that Kipling glorified, with the devotion that he sought to evoke on its behalf, has fallen irrevocably apart. Mandalay is now associated with an important Allied reverse during the second world war, and a whole civilization was endangered by a short battle fought out on the very road that symbolized so much romance for Kipling. And it is not irrelevant to mention these mundane considerations, in a way that would be quite out of place in the case of Marlowe's glorification of a nascent capitalism; because Kipling's writing proceeds on the level of the ephemeral, and as a journalist none of his work achieves that artistic detachment from the actual which alone could make his ideas live as Marlowe's live. And one can, in passing, only deplore that Mr. Eliot should have supposed that Kipling is in some way worthy of attention (not only, one presumes, literary attention), and that we should be invited to admire the writings of a man who speaks of the troops as revealing "the intense selfishness of the lower classes," of officers whose virtue consists in God's having "arranged that a clean-run youth of the British middle classes shall, in the matter of backbone, brains, and bowels, surpass all other youths," and who says of the battle in which they are engaged that "the bucketing went forward merrily"; but Mr. Eliot seems not to be acquainted with this aspect of Kipling.

Kipling's affiliations with the literary decadence are evident in his interest in language. The inventories of gems or scents or colours that one finds in Wilde are matched by his inventories and descriptions of mechanical components. As Théophile Gautier said, "the decadent style is the last effort of language to express everything to the last extremity," and this accurately describes Kipling, too. His verse and his prose are very carefully put together, and Mr. Eliot observes that he "could manage even so difficult a form as the sestina." Moreover, it is perfectly true that Kipling had a knack of turning a phrase quite as effectively as Shaw or Whistler; he shared with them the contemporary love of verbal dexterity, and he had the advantage over them of possessing a vulgarer mind, a mind closer to the communal platitude. With the result that it is Kipling, rather

than the accredited conversationalists of the decadence, who
has added to our language so many of those "toothsome amal-
gams of Americanisms and epigrams" that in some quarters
are thought so rare an acquisition.

But perhaps the most significant fact about the *fin-de-siècle*
writers was their spiritual isolation. Nearly all of them, in greater
or less degree, were sexually abnormal, and the eroticism of
much of their writing, and their endless quest after elaborate
sensation, masked an inner disorder and desolation whose real
nature they fought to conceal. The whole conduct of their lives,
with its affectation of dandyism and elaborate inconsequence,
was a device, perhaps subconsciously practised to a great extent, to make tolerable a lack of personal contact with others.
Whether it be in the writings of Wilde or Beerbohm, Francis
Thompson or Davidson, or even Bernard Shaw, the same un-
easiness is evident, and they all reveal a similar lack of confidence in the validity of individual relationships. Indeed, the
Ivory Tower was less an island of art standing out of a sea of
social activity than the very person of the isolated individual
himself. And in this connexion it is important to remember
how many of the dandies of the decadence ended their lives in
the sanctuary of the Roman Catholic Church; the organization
and the ritual enabled them to reconcile a longing for participation with a dependence on emotional indulgence. And it is
impossible to read any quantity of Kipling's verse and prose
without realizing immediately how similar was his case. "What
distinguished Kipling from so many present-day writers," says
Dr. Bonamy Dobrée (in *The Lamp and the Lute*), "is precisely
that he does not attempt to break down man's loneliness, seeing
only futility in the balm of the 'personal relation.'" The moral
of the tale "As Easy as A B C" is that democracy implies soli-
darity and co-operation; the only reply to this aberration is to
"Order the guns and kill!" and then to retire in on oneself
again. Unfortunately, this blissful after-condition is threatened
by a sudden resurrection of democracy, "and when once it's a
question of invasion of privacy, good-bye to right and reason
in Illinois!" The same symptom is treated more pretentiously
in one of the psychological tales, "In the Same Boat," where
the drug-addicts only escape into normality by pooling their

moral resources and struggling together against the recurrent crises. But Kipling emphasizes not so much their mutual dependence on each other's help as that such co-operation is strictly conditional on their mental disorder. When they manage to reach normality, their sense of joint effort and attraction, which alone had enabled them to achieve it, vanish, and "for the new-found life of him Conroy could not feel one flutter of instinct or emotion that turned to herward." And in a somewhat similar story, "The Brushwood Boy," the hero, whose "school was not encouraged to dwell on its emotions," only becomes inveigled into a love-affair as a result of repeated telepathic communications with the lady in question; and when, eventually, they meet and have to go through with it (or rather Kipling has to go through with it), the dialogue is arch and almost embarrassing in its artificiality. In fact, it was not that Kipling was isolated willingly or without regret, for one finds throughout his work the gravitation of one individual to another, even if this is described as the outcome of something abnormal; rather does one feel that an inner disability compelled him to this detachment from human sympathies, and that by way of compensation he forcibly identified himself with the larger structure of the British Empire and later of the English tradition. The sentiments that might normally have fastened on individuals were frustrated, and so they drove Kipling almost frantically, and quite obstinately, into participation in the great abstraction. As others have pointed out, Kipling took his imperialism not only seriously but even religiously, and it gave him the security and also the emotional outlet that we have noticed in the conversion to Rome of the dandies. Nothing is so typically decadent about Kipling as this spiritual isolation, and Mr. Dobrée has justly remarked (though to illustrate quite another point) that the Empire is Kipling's Catholic Church.

And this brings one to the second of the two issues fundamental to an understanding of Kipling, and it bears directly on all that has been said so far. For Kipling's journalism, his interest in the craft of writing, his isolation, and his religious attachment to the Empire are all fundamentally related to what I defined earlier as an atrophy of feeling. In his essay Mr. Eliot points out that "the changes in his poetry, while they cannot be explained by any usual scheme of poetic development, can to some extent be explained by changes in his outward circumstances," and elsewhere he confesses that "the critical tools which we are accustomed to use in analysing and criticising poetry do not seem to work." And this leads Mr. Eliot to offer a number of explanations of which even he seems sceptical: such as the theory that Kipling, as distinct from other poets, intends his poems "to *act*," or the theory, nowhere demonstrated, that he is "an integral prose-and-verse writer." But, were it not damaging to his general case, Mr. Eliot must surely have realized that development in art, and its critical analysis, is a matter of *emotional* growth, both extensively and intensively. And this is precisely what one fails to find either in Kipling's work as a whole or in his individual poems and stories. Like *Kim*, they are "things imposed from without," most often unfolding a given situation or panorama. And this lack of internal development gives even his most dramatic tales a certain dustiness in the mouth; the gritty detachment of the style and the flashes of emotionalism are not controlled by any sense of artistic logic, but proceed from a mind of set ideas and narrow sympathies. In fact, as one studies his life, one sees Kipling moving from prejudice to prejudice, from one tactlessness to another, and one cannot see even in his private affairs any accession of maturity or judgment. This debility he shares, as has been suggested, with the other writers of the decadence; and, as in their case, this throttling (and I feel it was not altogether a personal responsibility) of normal spontaneity of feeling was accompanied by an increasing concern with the mere machine of his art. To Mr. Edmund Wilson (see *The Wound and the Bow*) this appears puzzling: "It is the paradox of Kipling's career that he should have extended the conquests of his craftsmanship in proportion to the shrinking of the range of his dramatic imagination. As his responses to human beings became duller, his sensitivity to his medium increased." But there is no paradox in this, so long as one is not deceived by Kipling's "conquests of his craftsmanship." Personally I find his skill no more remarkable than Somerset Maugham's or H. G. Wells's; indeed, it rapidly developed into a formula that is all too easily and frequently copied. In very little of his work does one feel that he is doing much more than send his polished machine along the railroad that suits his whim of the moment; certainly it is a well-oiled and powerful locomotive, and it draws its freight of inanimate ideas and inanimate individuals unerringly to a pre-arranged destination; but of its nature it keeps to its rails and observes the dictation of a time-table.

One of the inevitable outcomes of Kipling's lack of warm-blooded feeling (as distinct from his susceptibility to full-blooded emotion) is that his interest centres in things and ideas, and the internal working of his individuals is treated as a process distinct from character and personality. Seldom does one find any suggestion of innate life; the Irish Mulvaney, the Scots M'Turk, the Anglo-Indian Mrs. Hauksbee, the American Zigler, or Pallant the English M.P., as well as the McAndrews and the troopers of the verse, are all of them actors on a carefully prepared stage-set; it is the drama they perform, rather than their own potentialities, that gives the story interest. And this explains the fact that Kipling appears to have had not much more interest in the thoughts and feelings of human beings than of animals and machines, or even in a pillow called Aunt Ellen. If one readily admits the virtuosity of the performance (for this seems simpler than to be niggling over such a triviality), yet one is still baffled to explain the interest in such stories as "The Maltese Cat" and ".007"; they only exemplify the kind of vulgarity that results from a concentration on the thing in itself. The whole undertaking was factitious; Kipling knew nothing at first hand about machines or animals, and his interest in them is essentially that of the advertising journalist who eventually "falls" for his own wares. And this enthusiasm for the machine, this interest in relationships in the abstract, is something quite different from the contemporary school of pylon-poets. It is one of the refuges of the shrinking sensibility and carries little or no social significance. And the other side to this escape into the inanimate is Kipling's resort to hysteria; the two attitudes represent complementary evasions of the problem of normal sympathetic existence.

The element of hysteria is pervasive. In one or two stories Kipling gets near to treating a story honestly, looking at its full-face; in "Without Benefit of Clergy," for instance, the re-

lationship between the British official and the Indian girl is almost satisfying. But at the crucial moment Kipling looks away;
fever and cholera carry off the girl and her child, and violence
breaks into what now seems to have been no more than an
indulgent day-dream. Either some violent happening is brought
in to shatter the glimpsed normality, or else Kipling dispenses
with even the glimpses of normality, and presents instead various
forms or aberration. On the most harmless level this takes the
form of the practical joke. *Stalky and Co.* can be accepted, if
only with difficulty, because one fondly supposes that most
things are possible with the adolescent; but Kipling soon aban-
dons even this degree of plausibility, and one finds exactly the
same conduct glorified in the Regimental Mess. In "The Tie,"
five officers beat up the civilian caterer, and this conduct is
justified because all of them have been to the same school and
thus his catering offence has disgraced not only the Mess but
also the Alma Mater; and the tale ends with one of the officers
"thinking over the moral significance of Old School ties and the
British Social fabric." Or there is "The Honours of War," in
which an officer, who has been assaulted by his brother officers
for being serious about military theory, decides not to take
ordinary action against the offenders; instead "he cast away all
shadow of his legal rights for the sake of a common or bear-
garden rag—such a rag as if it came to the ears of the authorities
would cost him his commission. They were saved, and their
saviour was their equal and their brother. So they chaffed and
reviled him as such, till he again squashed the breath out of
them, and we others laughed louder than they." Kipling seemed
to value above all irresponsibility as between individuals (of the
same sex, of course), perhaps as a relief from the tension of
observing unquestioning loyalty to the Idea. And in "The Village That Voted the Earth Was Flat" his boyish thrill in the
practical joke runs riot; the whole apparatus of the press, of
advertising, and of the music-hall is manipulated to wreak
vengeance on the offending Blimp, and in the end even the
House of Commons has succumbed, "hysterical and abandoned." But the thing to observe about this apparently harmless
taste for the practical joke, about these extravaganzas on group
irresponsibility and self-release, is that beneath it all there

smoulders a potentiality for individual hysteria. A very large
number of the tales deal with the mind on the edge of madness.
Some of them are ordinary enough, and in "The Woman in
His Life" the patient recovers as a result of developing a mawk-
ish affection for a dog. (In contrast to Lawrence, Kipling had
the kind of psychological insight that one picks up second-hand
in the smoke-room.) But most often these tales are not in the
least harmless, and Kipling's taste for hysteria seems to uncover
a deep longing for some similar violence of feeling in himself,
some means of escaping into the ideal life of ruthless activity.
Mr. Eliot is very wide of the point when he supposes that only
"those who do not believe in the existence of the Beast probably
consider 'The Mark of the Beast' a beastly story." This tale
seems to me beastly (surely the pun was unnecessary), not because one disbelieves in the Beast, but because Kipling's attitude towards it is so equivocal. One cannot avoid feeling that
he is mainly concerned with the opportunities for violent description that the Beast theme offers, and also with the element
of revenge that, so school-boyish an amusement in the tales
already discussed, gradually emerges as a major principle in his
philosophy. The leper, in this story, has branded Fleete with
the mark of the beast, and gradually it transforms him altogether
into a beast; in order to restore him back to humanity, the
leper is captured and forced by torture to eradicate the mark.
But the emphasis at the climax is all on the torture, and after
carefully describing the instruments used, Kipling resorts melo-
dramatically to a row of periods: "Strickland shaded his eyes
with his hands for a moment and then we got to work. This part
is not to be printed. . . ." And one retains a feeling that ruthlessness is the only solution and that revenge with violence is
sweet.

Of course, for Kipling revenge *is* sweet, and most of his tales
turn on feelings of revenge. In "Mary Postgate" Kipling writes
with less detachment than in any of his tales that I have read.
And as illustrating many of the points I have been making, this
story is worth consideration. Mary Postgate has been for a
long time governess to Fowler, who joins up in the Flying Corps
and is immediately killed on a trial flight; she comments: "It's
a great pity he didn't die in action after he had killed some-

body." She decides to burn all his belongings, and there follows
one of Kipling's interminable and tasteless inventories, occupying
a full page, describing the possessions that she collects for his
pyre; the sense of loss is gradually intensified through this emphasis on the inanimate object, giving a hard, unsympathetic
feeling to the proceeding. Mary Postgate then goes out for a
walk and is present when a bomb dropped by a German plane
kills a small girl. She returns to light her bonfire, and there,
sitting at the foot of a tree with a broken back, is the pilot of the
German machine which has just crashed.

The story, as can be seen at once, is internally quite bogus;
the whole thing is manipulated from the outside and for precon-
ceived purposes. The remaining pages simply describe the
ecstasy of Mary Postgate as she waits to hear the death-rattle of
the Germain airman. In spite of the earlier comment, she now
repeats to herself that "Wynn was a gentleman who for no consideration would have torn little Edna into those vividly
coloured strips and strings"; and so she waits, refusing the man
any help, until with an "increasing rapture" she perceives the
end is near, and then "she closed her eyes and drank it in," smiling. The importance of this is, I think, twofold. Kipling quite
candidly, like Mary Postgate, "ceased to think, and gave himself up to feel" when he undertook this story; and it seems as if
he had always been ready to indulge his feelings of revenge and
hysteria when he could. But, unfortunately for him, the opportunity could only seldom arise for a man who, like himself, had
done little but dip his pen into experiences of this kind. And
this, the second interesting factor, explains why the story operates through the agency of a woman. On the whole, Kipling
despised women; but in one or two tales he is glad to use them
to vent feelings that he would be ashamed to attribute to a
man, and above all to describe as being possible to himself. And
one feels, in this story, that he is quite conscious of vicarious
enjoyment in dealing with a woman whom he can safely allow
to be contradictory and irrational.

Always devoid of finer feeling and emotional discipline, Kipling here virtually extols these blemishes and, through the
medium of Mary Postgate's calculated indulgence, turns the
crude sensation over lovingly in his mouth. In this tale he does

openly what for the most part he holds down by means of the harsh he-man pose. And in this respect he is not only one of the founders of modern journalism, but also of the modern school of literary toughness. Kipling's contemporary counterpart is Hemingway, who writes up-to-date Kiplingese, and who betrays, beneath the staccato, machine-like prose, a similar coarseness of feeling that tends towards sentimentality on the one hand and towards brutishness on the other. What Kipling reveals, in every line he wrote, is a sensibility entirely devoid of moral discipline and artistic honesty; the only discipline he observes is that of his ideal Subaltern, the product of a "school that was not encouraged to dwell on its emotions, but rather to keep in hard condition, and to avoid false quantities." It is in products of this kind of training that one finds, almost invariably, an outward tough obstinacy protecting a soft centre of self-distrust and potential hysteria.

To go further into the matter, or to support these generalizations with detailed analysis, would be to perform a task out of all importance to its intrinsic importance. Kipling, in fact, seems to me neither so disgusting, for the most part, as he has been painted, nor worth the interest that Mr. Eliot seeks to encourage. And this particularly applies to his verse. Mr. Eliot admits to knowing no writer "for whom poetry seems to have been more purely an instrument"; and the uses to which this instrument was put are no longer likely to be of much appeal today. We do not, on the whole, visualize the future "in the shape of a semi-circle of buildings and temples projecting into a sea of dreams," which for Kipling represented "the whole sweep and meaning of things and effort and origins throughout the Empire"; and the experience on which we work as social historians is not likely to be limited to the volumes of *Punch*, "from whose files I drew my modern working history."

In the end it is rather distressing to find Mr. Eliot advocating a revival of interest in such a writer. Of course, one can see the attraction that Kipling might have for him: for Kipling was the popular success that Mr. Eliot will never be, he was anti-Liberal with a crude gusto that Mr. Eliot can never attempt to equal, and above all he rested within the Catholic Church of his Empire with a solid assurance and with a sense of fulfilment that

will always be artistically denied to Mr. Eliot in his dealings
with the Anglican brotherhood. If Mr. Eliot has been undoubtedly the most important name in literature during the period
between the two wars, this has entailed a sacrifice that he seems
decreasingly willing to make; that side of him which confesses to
a taste for music-hall and Camembert, for cats and for Douglas
Credit—in short, his strain of the dilettante, even, one might
say, of the decadent—leads him to look wistfully at the confident
and unabashed vulgarity of Kipling. Perhaps, above all, it is
this unattainable mastery and this security within the envelop-
ing aura of the larger structure that appeals to one so fraught
with doubt and insecurity, to one who has spoken of "twenty
years largely wasted" trying, with every attempt "a different
kind of failure," to "learn to use new words;" spoken of the
fight "to recover what has been lost/And found and lost again
and again. . . ." Kipling lacked this kind of honesty and hence
he lacked any sense of this kind of problem; through a partly
deliberate thickening of the hide he convinced himself that
"The game is more than the player of the game,/And the ship
is more than the crew." In his poetry, at least, Mr. Eliot has
never sought refuge by renouncing the integrity of his personal
response and the guidance of his matured sensibility; and up to
the present he has not succumbed to the appeal of the Thing
and of the System, the lure of the Ship and the Game.

George Orwell

Rudyard Kipling *

IT WAS a pity that Mr. Eliot should be so much on the defensive
in the long essay with which he prefaces this selection of Kipling's poetry, but it was not to be avoided, because before one
can even speak about Kipling one has to clear away a legend
that has been created by two sets of people who have not read
his works. Kipling is in the peculiar position of having been a
byword for fifty years. During five literary generations every enlightened person has despised him, and at the end of that time
nine-tenths of those enlightened persons are forgotten and Kipling is in some sense still there. Mr. Eliot never satisfactorily
explains this fact, because in answering the shallow and familiar
charge that Kipling is a "fascist," he falls into the opposite
error of defending him where he is not defensible. It is no use
pretending that Kipling's view of life, as a whole, can be accepted or even forgiven by any civilised person. It is no use claiming, for instance, that when Kipling describes a British soldier
beating a "nigger" with a cleaning rod in order to get money out
of him, he is acting merely as a reporter and does not necessarily
approve what he describes. There is not the slightest sign anywhere in Kipling's work that he disapproves of that kind of
conduct—on the contrary, there is a definite strain of sadism in
him, over and above the brutality which a writer of that type
has to have. Kipling *is* a jingo imperialist, he *is* morally insensi-

* [From *Dickens, Dali and Others* (New York, 1946). First published
in 1942, revised in 1945. Reprinted by permission of Harcourt, Brace &
World, Inc. and Martin Secker & Warburg, Ltd.]

tive and aesthetically disgusting. It is better to start by admitting
that, and then to try to find out why it is that he survives while
the refined people who have sniggered at him seem to wear so
badly.

And yet the "fascist" charge has to be answered, because the
first clue to any understanding of Kipling, morally or politically,
is the fact that he was *not* a fascist. He was further from being
one than the most humane or the most "progressive" person is
able to be nowadays. An interesting instance of the way in which
quotations are parroted to and fro without any attempt to
look up their context or discover their meaning is the line from
"Recessional," "Lesser breeds without the Law." This line is
always good for a snigger in pansy-left circles. It is assumed as
a matter of course that the "lesser breeds" are "natives," and a
mental picture is called up of some *pukka sahib* in a pith helmet
kicking a coolie. In its context the sense of the line is almost the
exact opposite of this. The phrase "lesser breeds" refers almost
certainly to the Germans, and especially the pan-German writers,
who are "without the Law" in the sense of being lawless, not in
the sense of being powerless. The whole poem, conventionally
thought of as an orgy of boasting, is a denunciation of power
politics, British as well as German. Two stanzas are worth quoting (I am quoting this as politics, not as poetry):

> If, drunk with sight of power, we loose
>   Wild tongues that have not Thee in awe,
> Such boastings as the Gentiles use,
>   Or lesser breeds without the Law—
> Lord God of Hosts, be with us yet,
> Lest we forget—lest we forget!
>
> For heathen heart that puts her trust
>   In reeking tube and iron shard,
> All valiant dust that builds on dust,
>   And guarding, calls not Thee to guard,
> For frantic boast and foolish word—
> Thy mercy on Thy people, Lord!

Much of Kipling's phraseology is taken from the Bible, and
no doubt in the second stanza he had in mind the text from
Psalm cxxvii: "Except the Lord build the house, they labour in
vain that build it; except the Lord keep the city, the watchman

waketh but in vain." It is not a text that makes much impression on the post-Hitler mind. No one, in our time, believes in any sanction greater than military power; no one believes that it is possible to overcome force except by greater force. There is no "law," there is only power. I am not saying that that is a true belief, merely that it is the belief which all modern men do actually hold. Those who pretend otherwise are either intellectual cowards, or power-worshippers under a thin disguise, or have simply not caught up with the age they are living in. Kipling's outlook is pre-fascist. He still believes that pride comes before a fall and that the gods punish *hubris*. He does not foresee the tank, the bombing plane, the radio and the secret police, or their psychological results.

But in saying this, does not one unsay what I said above about Kipling's jingoism and brutality? No, one is merely saying that the nineteenth-century imperialist outlook and the modern gangster outlook are two different things. Kipling belongs very definitely to the period 1885–1902. The Great War and its aftermath embittered him, but he shows little sign of having learned anything from any event later than the Boer War. He was the prophet of British Imperialism in its expansionist phase (even more than his poems, his solitary novel, *The Light that Failed*, gives you the atmosphere of that time) and also the unofficial historian of the British Army, the old mercenary army which began to change its shape in 1914. All his confidence, his bouncing vulgar vitality, sprang out of limitations which no fascist or near-fascist shares.

Kipling spent the later part of his life in sulking, and no doubt it was political disappointment rather than literary vanity that accounted for this. Somehow history had not gone according to plan. After the greatest victory she had ever known, Britain was a lesser world power than before, and Kipling was quite acute enough to see this. The virtue had gone out of the classes he idealised, the young were hedonistic or disaffected, the desire to paint the map red had evaporated. He could not understand what was happening, because he had never had any grasp of the economic forces underlying imperial expansion. It is notable that Kipling does not seem to realise, any more than the average soldier or colonial administrator, that an empire is primarily a money-making concern. Imperialism as he sees it is a sort of forcible evangelising. You turn a Gatling gun on a mob of un- armed "natives," and then you establish "the Law," which in- cludes roads, railways and a court-house. He could not foresee, therefore, that the same motives which brought the Empire into existence would end by destroying it. It was the same motive, for example, that caused the Malayan jungles to be cleared for rubber estates, and which now causes those estates to be handed over intact to the Japanese. The modern totalitarians know what they are doing, and the nineteenth-century English did not know what they were doing. Both attitudes have their advan- tages, but Kipling was never able to move forward from one into the other. His outlook, allowing for the fact that after all he was an artist, was that of the salaried bureaucrat who despises the "box wallah" and often lives a lifetime without realising that the "box wallah" calls the tune.

But because he identifies himself with the official class, he does possess one thing which "enlightened" people seldom or never possess, and that is a sense of responsibility. The middle- class Left hate him for this quite as much as for his cruelty and vulgarity. All left-wing parties in the highly industrialised coun- tries are at bottom a sham, because they make it their business to fight against something which they do not really wish to destroy. They have internationalist aims, and at the same time they struggle to keep up a standard of life with which those aims are incompatible. We all live by robbing Asiatic coolies, and those of us who are "enlightened" all maintain that those coolies ought to be set free; but our standard of living, and hence our "enlightenment," demands that the robbery shall continue. A humanitarian is always a hypocrite, and Kipling's understand- ing of this is perhaps the central secret of his power to create telling phrases. It would be difficult to hit off the one-eyed pacifism of the English in fewer words than in the phrase, "making mock of uniforms that guard you while you sleep." It is true that Kipling does not understand the economic aspect of the relationship between the highbrow and the blimp. He does not see that the map is painted red chiefly in order that the coolie may be exploited. Instead of the coolie he sees the Indian Civil Servant; but even on that plane his grasp of function, of who protects whom, is very sound. He sees clearly that men can only be highly civilised while other men, inevitably less civilised, are there to guard and feed them.

How far does Kipling really identify himself with the administrators, soldiers and engineers whose praises he sings? Not so completely as is sometimes assumed. He had travelled very widely while he was still a young man, he had grown up with a brilliant mind in mainly philistine surroundings, and some streak in him that may have been partly neurotic led him to prefer the active man to the sensitive man. The nineteenth-century Anglo-Indians, to name the least sympathetic of his idols, were at any rate people who did things. It may be that all that they did was evil, but they changed the face of the earth (it is instructive to look at a map of Asia and compare the railway system of India with that of the surrounding countries), whereas they could have achieved nothing, could not have maintained themselves in power for a single week, if the normal Anglo-Indian outlook had been that of, say, E. M. Forster. Tawdry and shallow though it is, Kipling's is the only literary picture that we possess of nineteenth-century Anglo-India, and he could only make it because he was just coarse enough to be able to exist and keep his mouth shut in clubs and regimental messes. But he did not greatly resemble the people he admired. I know from several private sources that many of the Anglo-Indians who were Kipling's contemporaries did not like or approve of him. They said, no doubt truly, that he knew nothing about India, and on the other hand, he was from their point of view too much of a highbrow. While in India he tended to mix with "the wrong" people, and because of his dark complexion he was wrongly suspected of having a streak of Asiatic blood. Much in his development is traceable to his having been born in India and having left school early. With a slightly different background he might have been a good novelist or a superlative writer of music-hall songs. But how true is it that he was a vulgar flag-waver, a sort of publicity agent for Cecil Rhodes? It is true, but it is not true that he was a yes-man or a time-server. After his early days, if then, he never courted public opinion. Mr. Eliot says that what is held against him is that he expressed unpopular views in a popular style. This narrows the issue by assuming that "unpopular" means unpopular with the intelligentsia, but it is a fact that Kipling's "message" was one that the big public did not want, and, indeed, has never accepted. The mass of the people, in the 'nineties as now, were anti-militarist, bored by the Empire and only unconsciously patriotic. Kipling's official admirers are and were the "service" middle class, the people who read *Blackwood's*. In the stupid early years of this century, the blimps, having at last discovered some- one who could be called a poet and who was on their side, set Kipling on a pedestal, and some of his more sententious poems, such as "If," were given almost Biblical status. But it is doubtful whether the blimps have ever read him with attention, any more than they have read the Bible. Much of what he says they could not possibly approve. Few people who have criticised England from the inside have said bitterer things about her than this gutter patriot. As a rule it is the British working class that he is attacking, but not always. That phrase about "the flannelled fools at the wicket and the muddied oafs at the goal" sticks like an arrow to this day, and it is aimed at the Eton and Harrow match as well as the Cup-Tie Final. Some of the verses he wrote about the Boer War have a curiously modern ring, so far as their subject-matter goes. "Stellenbosch," which must have been written about 1902, sums up what every intelligent infantry officer was saying in 1918, or is saying now, for that matter.

Kipling's romantic ideas about England and the Empire might not have mattered if he could have held them without having the class-prejudices which at that time went with them. If one examines his best and most representative work, his soldier poems, especially *Barrack-Room Ballads*, one notices that what more than anything else spoils them is an underlying air of patronage. Kipling idealises the army officer, especially the junior officer, and that to an idiotic extent, but the private soldier, though lovable and romantic, has to be a comic. He is always made to speak in a sort of stylised cockney, not very broad but with all the aitches and final "g's" carefully omitted. Very often the result is as embarrassing as the humorous recitation at a church social. And this accounts for the curious fact that one can often improve Kipling's poems, make them less facetious

and less blatant by simply going through them and transplant-
ing them from cockney into standard speech. This is especially
true of his refrains, which often have a truly lyrical quality. Two
examples will do (one is about a funeral and the other about a
wedding):

> So it's knock out your pipes and follow me!
> And it's finish up your swipes and follow me!
> Oh, hark to the big drum calling,
> Follow me—follow me home!

and again:

> Cheer for the Sergeant's wedding—
> Give them one cheer more!
> Grey gun-horses in the lando,
> And a rogue is married to a whore!

Here I have restored the aitches, etc. Kipling ought to have
known better. He ought to have seen that the two closing lines
of the first of these stanzas are very beautiful lines, and that
ought to have overridden his impulse to make fun of a working-
man's accent. In the ancient ballads the lord and the peasant
speak the same language. This is impossible to Kipling, who is
looking down a distorting class-perspective, and by a piece of
poetic justice one of his best lines is spoiled—for "follow me
'ome" is much uglier than "follow me home." But even where
it makes no difference musically the facetiousness of his stage
cockney dialect is irritating. However, he is more often quoted
aloud than read on the printed page, and most people instinctively make the necessary alterations when they quote him.

Can one imagine any private soldier, in the 'nineties or now,
reading *Barrack-Room Ballads* and feeling that here was a writer
who spoke for him? It is very hard to do so. Any soldier capable
of reading a book of verse would notice at once that Kipling is
almost unconscious of the class war that goes on in an army
as much as elsewhere. It is not only that he thinks the soldier
comic, but that he thinks him patriotic, feudal, a ready admirer
of his officers, and proud to be a soldier of the Queen. Of
course that is partly true, or battles could not be fought, but
"What have I done for thee, England, my England?" is essentially a middle-class query. Almost any working man would

follow it up immediately with "What has England done for me?" In so far as Kipling grasps this, he simply sets it down to "the intense selfishness of the lower classes" (his own phrase). When he is writing not of British but of "loyal" Indians he carries the "Salaam, sahib" *motif* to sometimes disgusting lengths. Yet it remains true that he has far more interest in the common soldier, far more anxiety that he shall get a fair deal, than most of the "liberals" of his day or our own. He sees that the soldier is neglected, meanly underpaid, and hypocritically despised by the people whose income he safeguards. "I came to realise," he says in his posthumous memoirs, "the bare horrors of the private's life, and the unnecessary torments he endured." He is accused of glorifying war, and perhaps he does so, but not in the usual manner, by pretending that war is a sort of football match. Like most people capable of writing battle poetry, Kipling had never been in battle, but his vision of war is realistic. He knows that bullets hurt, that under fire everyone is terrified, that the ordinary soldier never knows what the war is about or what is happening except in his own corner of the battlefield, and that British troops, like other troops, frequently run away:

> I 'erd the knives be'ind me, but I dursn't face my man,
>   Nor I don't know where I went to, 'cause I didn't 'alt to see,
> Till I 'eard a beggar squealin' out for quarter as 'e ran,
>   An' I thought I knew the voice an'—it was me!

Modernise the style of this, and it might have come out of one of the debunking war books of the nineteen-twenties. Or again:

> An' now the hugly bullets come peckin' through the dust,
> An' no one wants to face 'em, but every beggar must;
> So, like a man in irons, which isn't glad to go,
> They moves 'em off by companies uncommon stiff and slow.

Compare this with:

> Forward the Light Brigade!
> Was there a man dismayed?
> No! though the soldier knew
> Someone had blundered.

If anything, Kipling overdoes the horrors, for the wars of his youth were hardly wars at all by our standards. Perhaps that is due to the neurotic strain in him, the hunger for cruelty. But at least he knows that men ordered to attack impossible objectives *are* dismayed, and also that fourpence a day is not a generous pension.

How complete or truthful a picture has Kipling left us of the long-service, mercenary army of the late nineteenth century? One must say of this, as of what Kipling wrote about nineteenth century Anglo-India, that it is not only the best but almost the only literary picture we have. He has put on record an immense amount of stuff that one could otherwise only gather from verbal tradition or from unreadable regimental histories. Perhaps his picture of army life seems fuller and more accurate than it is because any middle-class English person is likely to know enough to fill up the gaps. At any rate, reading the essay on Kipling that Mr. Edmund Wilson has just published or is just about to publish, I was struck by the number of things that are boringly familiar to us and seem to be barely intelligible to an American. But from the body of Kipling's early work there does seem to emerge a vivid and not seriously misleading picture of the old pre-machine-gun army—the sweltering barracks in Gibraltar or Lucknow, the red coats, the pipeclayed belts and the pillbox hats, the beer, the fights, the floggings, hangings and crucifixions, the bugle-calls, the smell of oats and horse-piss, the bellowing sergeants with foot-long moustaches, the bloody skirmishes, invariably mismanaged, the crowded troopships, the cholera-stricken camps, the "native" concubines, the ultimate death in the workhouse. It is a crude, vulgar picture in which a patriotic music-hall turn seems to have got mixed up with one of Zola's gorier passages, but from it future generations will be able to gather some idea of what a long-term volunteer army was like. On about the same level they will be able to learn something of British India in the days when motor-cars and refrigerators were unheard of. It is an error to imagine that we might have had better books on these subjects if, for example, George Moore, or Gissing, or Thomas Hardy, had had Kipling's opportunities. That is the kind of accident that cannot happen. It was not possible that nineteenth-century England should produce a book like *War and Peace*, or like Tolstoy's minor stories of army life, such as "Sebastopol" or "The Cossacks," not because the talent was necessarily lacking but because no one with sufficient sensitiveness to write such books would ever have made the appropriate contacts. Tolstoy lived in a great military empire in which it seemed natural for almost any young man of family to spend a few years in the army, whereas the British Empire was and still is demilitarised to a degree which Continental observers find almost incredible. Civilised men do not readily move away from the centres of civilisation, and in most languages there is a great dearth of what one might call colonial literature. It took a very improbable combination of circumstances to produce Kipling's gaudy tableau, in which Private Ortheris and Mrs. Hauksbee pose against a background of palm trees to the sound of temple bells, and one necessary circumstance was that Kipling himself was only half civilised.

Kipling is the only English writer of our time who has added phrases to the language. The phrases and neologisms which we take over and use without remembering their origins do not always come from writers we admire. It is strange, for instance, to hear Nazi broadcasters referring to the Russian soldiers as "robots," thus unconsciously borrowing a word from a Czech democrat whom they would have killed if they could have laid hands on him. Here are half a dozen phrases coined by Kipling which one sees quoted in leaderettes in the gutter Press or overhears in saloon bars from people who have barely heard his name. It will be seen that they all have a certain characteristic in common:

> East is East, and West is West.
> The white man's burden.
> What do they know of England who only England know?
> The female of the species is more deadly than the male.
> Somewhere East of Suez.
> Paying the Dane-geld.

There are various others, including some that have outlived their context by many years. The phrase "killing Kruger with your mouth," for instance, was current till very recently. It is also possible that it was Kipling who first let loose the use of the word "Huns" for Germans; at any rate he began using it as soon as the guns opened fire in 1914. But what the phrases I have listed above have in common is that they are all of them phrases which one utters semi-derisively (as it might be "For I'm to be Queen o' the May, mother, I'm to be Queen o' the May"), but which one is bound to make use of sooner or later. Nothing could exceed the contempt of the *New Statesman*, for instance, for Kipling, but how many times during the Munich period did the *New Statesman* find itself quoting that phrase about paying the Dane-geld? [1] The fact is that Kipling, apart from his snack-bar wisdom and his gift for packing much cheap picturesqueness into a few words ("Palm and Pine"—"East of Suez"—"The Road to Mandalay"), is generally talking about things that are of urgent interest. It does not matter, from this point of view, that thinking and decent people generally find themselves on the other side of the fence from him. "White man's burden" instantly conjures up a real problem, even if one feels that it ought to be altered to "black man's burden." One may disagree to the middle of one's bones with the political attitude implied in "The Islanders," but one cannot say that it is a frivolous attitude. Kipling deals in thoughts which are both vulgar and permanent. This raises the question of his special status as a poet, or verse-writer.

Mr. Eliot describes Kipling's metrical work as "verse" and not "poetry," but adds that it is "*great* verse," and further qualifies this by saying that a writer can only be described as a "great verse-writer" if there is some of his work "of which we cannot say whether it is verse or poetry." Apparently Kipling was a versifier who occasionally wrote poems, in which case it was a pity that Mr. Eliot did not specify these poems by name. The trouble is that whenever an aesthetic judgment on Kipling's work seems to be called for, Mr. Eliot is too much on the defensive to be able to speak plainly. What he does not say, and what I think one ought to start by saying in any discussion of

---

1 1945. On the first page of his recent book *Adam and Eve*, Mr. Middleton Murry quotes the well-known lines:

There are nine and sixty ways
Of constructing tribal lays,
And every single one of them is right.

He attributes these lines to Thackeray. This is probably what is known as a "Freudian error." A civilised person would prefer not to quote Kipling, *i.e.*, would prefer not to feel that it was Kipling who had expressed his thought for him.

Kipling, is that most of Kipling's verse is so horribly vulgar that it gives one the same sensation as one gets from watching a third-rate music-hall performer recite "The Pigtail of Wu Fang Fu" with the purple limelight on his face, *and yet* there is much of it that is capable of giving pleasure to people who know what poetry means. At his worst, and also his most vital, in poems like "Gunga Din" or "Danny Deever," Kipling is almost a shameful pleasure, like the taste for cheap sweets that some people secretly carry into middle life. But even with his best passages one has the same sense of being seduced by something spurious, and yet unquestionably seduced. Unless one is merely a snob and a liar it is impossible to say that no one who cares for poetry could get any pleasure out of such lines as:

For the wind is in the palm-trees, and the temple-bells they say:
"Come you back, you British soldier; come you back to Mandalay!"

and yet those lines are not poetry in the same sense as "Felix Randal" or "When icicles hang by the wall" are poetry. One can, perhaps, place Kipling more satisfactorily than by juggling with the words "verse" and "poetry," if one describes him simply as a good bad poet. He is as a poet what Harriet Beecher Stowe was as a novelist. And the mere existence of work of this kind, which is perceived by generation after generation to be vulgar and yet goes on being read, tells one something about the age we live in.

There is a great deal of good bad poetry in English, all of it, I should say, subsequent to 1790. Examples of good bad poems —I am deliberately choosing diverse ones—are "The Bridge of Sighs," "When all the World is Young, Lad," "The Charge of the Light Brigade," Bret Harte's "Dickens in Camp," "The Burial of Sir John Moore," "Jenny kissed me," "Keith of Ravelston," "Casabianca." All of these reek of sentimentality, and yet—not these particular poems, perhaps, but poems of this kind, are capable of giving true pleasure to people who can see clearly what is wrong with them. One could fill a fair-sized anthology with good bad poems, if it were not for the significant fact that good bad poetry is usually too well known to be worth reprinting. It is no use pretending that in an age like our own, "good" poetry can have any genuine popularity. It is, and must be, the cult of a very few people, the least tolerated of the arts. Perhaps that statement needs a certain amount of qualification. True poetry can sometimes be acceptable to the mass of the people when it disguises itself as something else. One can see an example of this in the folk-poetry that England still possesses, certain nursery rhymes and mnemonic rhymes, for instance, and the songs that soldiers make up, including the words that go to some of the bugle-calls. But in general ours is a civilisation in which the very word "poetry" evokes a hostile snigger or, at best, the sort of frozen disgust that most people feel when they hear the word "God." If you are good at playing the concertina you could probably go into the nearest public bar and get yourself an appreciative audience within five minutes. But what would be the attitude of that same audience if you suggested reading them Shakespeare's sonnets, for instance? Good bad poetry, however, can get across to the most unpromising audiences if the right atmosphere has been worked up beforehand. Some months back Churchill produced a great effect by quoting Clough's "Endeavor" in one of his broadcast speeches. I listened to this speech among people who could certainly not be accused of caring for poetry, and I am convinced that the lapse into verse impressed them and did not embarrass them. But not even Churchill could have got away with it if he had quoted anything much better than this.

In so far as a writer of verse can be popular, Kipling has been and probobly still is popular. In his own lifetime some of his poems travelled far beyond the bounds of the reading public, beyond the world of school prize-days, Boy Scout singsongs, limp-leather editions, poker-work and calendars, and out into the yet vaster world of the music halls. Nevertheless, Mr. Eliot thinks it worth while to edit him, thus confessing to a taste which others share but are not always honest enough to mention. The fact that such a thing as good bad poetry can exist is a sign of the emotional overlap between the intellectual and the ordinary man. The intellectual *is* different from the ordinary man, but only in certain sections of his personality, and even then not all the time. But what is the peculiarity of a good bad poem? A good bad poem is a graceful monument to the obvious. It records in memorable form—for verse is a mnemonic device, among other things—some emotion which very nearly every human being can share. The merit of a poem like "When all the World is Young, Lad" is that, however sentimental it may be, its sentiment is "true" sentiment in the sense that you are bound to find yourself thinking the thought it expresses sooner or later; and then, if you happen to know the poem, it will come back into your mind and seem better than it did before. Such poems are a kind of rhyming proverb, and it is a fact that definitely popular poetry is usually gnomic or sententious. One example from Kipling will do:

> White hands cling to the tightened rein,
>   Slipping the spur from the booted heel,
> Tenderest voices cry, "Turn again!"
>   Red lips tarnish the scabbarded steel. . . .
>
> Down to Gehenna or up to the Throne,
> He travels the fastest who travels alone.

There is a vulgar thought vigorously expressed. It may not be true, but at any rate it is a thought that everyone thinks. Sooner or later you will have occasion to feel that he travels the fastest who travels alone, and there the thought is, ready made and, as it were, waiting for you. So the chances are that, having once heard this line, you will remember it.

One reason for Kipling's power as a good bad poet I have already suggested—his sense of responsibility, which made it possible for him to have a world-view, even though it happened to be a false one. Although he had no direct connexion with any political party, Kipling was a conservative, a thing that does not exist nowadays. Those who now call themselves conservatives are either liberals, fascists or the accomplices of fascists. He identified himself with the ruling power and not with the opposition. In a gifted writer this seems to us strange and even disgusting, but it did have the advantage of giving Kipling a certain grip on reality. The ruling power is always faced with the question, "In such and such circumstances, what would you *do?*," whereas the opposition is not obliged to take responsibility or make any real decisions. Where it is a permanent and pensioned opposition, as in England, the quality of its thought deteriorates accordingly. Moreover, anyone who starts out with a pessimistic, reactionary view of life tends to be justified by events, for Utopia never arrives and "the gods of the copybook headings," as Kipling himself put it, always return. Kipling sold out to the British governing class, not financially but emotionally. This warped his political judgment, for the British ruling class were not what he imagined, and let him into abysses of folly and snobbery, but he gained a corresponding advantage from having at least tried to imagine what action and responsibility are like. It is a great thing in his favour that he is not witty, not "daring," has no wish to *épater les bourgeois*. He dealt largely in platitudes, and since we live in a world of platitudes, much of what he said sticks. Even his worst follies seem less shallow and less irritating than the "enlightened" utterances of the same period, such as Wilde's epigrams or the collection of cracker-mottoes at the end of *Man and Superman*.

Lionel Trilling
Kipling *

KIPLING BELONGS irrevocably to our past, and although the renewed critical attention he has lately been given by Edmund
Wilson and T. S. Eliot is friendlier and more interesting than
any he has received for a long time, it is less likely to make us
revise our opinions than to revive our memories of him. But
these memories, when revived, will be strong, for if Kipling
belongs to our past, he belongs there very firmly, fixed deep in
childhood feeling. And especially for liberals of a certain age he
must always be an interesting figure, for he had an effect upon
us in that obscure and important part of our minds where literary feeling and political attitude meet, an effect so much the
greater because it was so early experienced; and then for many of
us our rejection of him was our first literary-political decision.

My own relation with Kipling was intense and I believe
typical. It began, properly enough, with *The Jungle Books*. This
was my first independently chosen and avidly read book, my first
literary discovery, all the more wonderful because I had come
upon it in an adult "set," one of the ten green volumes of the
Century Edition that used to be found in many homes. (The
"set" has become unfashionable, and that is a blow to the literary education of the young, who, once they had been lured to an
author, used to remain loyal to him until they had read him by
the yard.) The satisfactions of *The Jungle Books* were large and

* [From *The Liberal Imagination* (New York, 1949). First published
in 1943. Copyright by the author. Reprinted by permission of The Viking
Press, Inc. and Martin Secker & Warburg, Ltd.]

numerous. I suppose a boy's vestigial animal totemism was pleased; there were the marvellous but credible abilities of Mowgli; there were the deadly enmities and grandiose revenges, strangely and tragically real. And it was a world peopled by wonderful parents, not only Mother Wolf and Father Wolf, but also—the fathers were far more numerous than the mothers— Bagheera the panther, Baloo the bear, Hathi the elephant, and the dreadful but decent Kaa the python, a whole council of strength and wisdom which was as benign as it was dangerous, and no doubt much of the delight came from discovering the benignity of this feral world. And then there was the fascination of the Pack and its Law. It is not too much to say that a boy had thus his first introduction to a generalized notion of society. It was a notion charged with feeling—the Law was mysterious, firm, certain, noble, in every way admirable beyond any rule of home or school.

Mixed up with this feeling about the Pack and the Law, and perfectly expressing it, was the effect of Kipling's gnomic language, both in prose and in verse, for you could not entirely skip the verse that turned up in the prose, and so you were led to trust yourself to the *Barrack Room Ballads* at a time when you would trust no other poetry. That gnomic quality of Kipling's, that knowing allusiveness which later came to seem merely vulgar, was, when first experienced, a delightful thing. By understanding Kipling's ellipses and allusions, you partook of what was Kipling's own special delight, the joy of being "in." Max Beerbohm has satirized Kipling's yearning to be admitted to any professional arcanum, his fawning admiration of the man in uniform, the man with the know-how and the technical slang. It is the emotion of a boy—he lusts for the exclusive circle, for the sect with the password, and he profoundly admires the technical, secret-laden adults who run the world, the overalled people, majestic in their occupation, superb in their preoccupation, the dour engineer and the thoughtful plumber. To this emotion, developed not much beyond a boy's, Kipling was addicted all his life, and eventually it made him silly and a bore. But a boy reading Kipling was bound to find all this sense of arcanum very pertinent; as, for example, it expressed itself in *Plain Tales from the Hills*, it seemed the very essence of adult

life. Kipling himself was not much more than a boy when he
wrote these remarkable stories—remarkable because, no matter
how one judges them, one never forgets the least of them—and
he saw the adult world as full of rites of initiation, of closed
doors and listeners behind them, councils, boudoir conferences,
conspiracies, innuendoes, and special knowledge. It was very
baffling, and certainly as an introduction to literature it went
counter to all our present educational theory, according to which
a child should not be baffled at all but should read only about
what he knows of from experience; but one worked it out by a
sort of algebra, one discovered the meaning of the unknowns
through the knowns, and just as one got without definition an
adequate knowledge of what a *sais* was, or a *dâk*-bungalow, and
what the significance of *pukka* was, so one penetrated to what
went on between the Gadsbys and to why Mrs. Hauksbee was
supposed to be charming and Mrs. Reiver not. Kipling's superior
cryptic tone was in effect an invitation to understand all this—it
suggested first that the secret was being kept not only from oneself but from everyone else and then it suggested that the
secret was not so much being kept as revealed, if one but guessed
hard enough. And this elaborate manner was an invitation to be
"in" not only on life but on literature; to follow its hints with
a sense of success was to become an initiate of literature, a Past
Master, a snob of the esoteric Mystery of the Word.

"Craft" and "craftily" were words that Kipling loved (no
doubt they were connected with his deep Masonic attachment),
and when he used them he intended all their several meanings
at once—shrewdness, a special technique, a special *secret* technique communicated by some master of it, and the bond that
one user of the technique would naturally have with another.
This feeling about the Craft, the Mystery, grew on Kipling and
colored his politics and even his cosmological ideas quite for
the worse, but to a boy it suggested the virtue of disinterested
professional commitment. If one ever fell in love with the cult
of art, it was not because one had been proselytized by some
intelligent Frenchman, but because one had absorbed Kipling's
credal utterances about the virtues of craft and had read *The
Light that Failed* literally to pieces.

These things we must be sure to put into the balance when we make up our account with Kipling—these and a few more. To a middle-class boy he gave a literary sanction for the admiration of the illiterate and shiftless parts of humanity. He was the first to suggest what may be called the anthropological view, the perception that another man's idea of virtue and honour may be different from one's own but quite to be respected. We must remember this when we condemn his mindless imperialism. Indians naturally have no patience whatever with Kipling and they condemn even his best book, *Kim*, saying that even here, where his devotion to the Indian life is most fully expressed, he falsely represents the Indians. Perhaps this is so, yet the dominant emotions of *Kim* are love and respect for the aspects of Indian life that the ethos of the West does not usually regard even with leniency. *Kim* established the value of things a boy was not likely to find approved anywhere else—the rank, greasy, over-rich things, the life that was valuable outside the notions of orderliness, success, and gentility. It suggested not only a multitude of different ways of life, but even different modes of thought. Thus, whatever one might come to feel personally about religion, a reading of *Kim* could not fail to establish religion's factual reality, not as piety, which was the apparent extent of its existence in the West, but as something at the very root of life; in *Kim*, one saw the myth in the making before one's very eyes and understood how and why it was made, and this, when later one had the intellectual good luck to remember it, had more to say about history and culture than anything in one's mere experience. *Kim*, like *The Jungle Books*, is full of wonderful fathers, all dedicated men in their different ways, each representing a different possibility of existence; and the charm of each is the greater because the boy need not commit himself to one alone but, like Kim himself, may follow Mahbub Ali into the shrewdness and sensuality of the bazaars, and be initiated by Colonel Creighton into the cold glamour of the Reason of State, and yet also make himself the son of the Lama, the very priest of contemplation and peace.

And then a boy in a large New York high school could find a blessed release from the school's offensive pieties about "service" and "character" in the scornful individualism of *Stalky & Co*. But it was with *Stalky & Co*. that the spell was broken, and significantly enough by H. G. Wells. In his *Outline of History*, Wells connected the doings of Stalky, M'Turk, and Beetle with British imperialism, and he characterized both in a way that made one see how much callousness, arrogance, and brutality one had been willing to accept. From then on the disenchantment grew. Exactly because Kipling was so involved with one's boyhood, one was quick to give him up in one's adolescence. The Wellsian liberalism took hold, and Shaw offered a new romance of wit and intellect. The new movements in literature came in to make Kipling seem inconsequential and puerile, to require that he be dismissed as official and, as one used to say, intending something aesthetic and emotional rather than political, "bourgeois." He ceased to be the hero of life and literature and became the villain, although even then a natural gratitude kept green the memory of the pleasure he had given.

But the world has changed a great deal since the days when that antagonism between Kipling and enlightenment was at its early intensity, and many intellectual and political things have shifted from their old assigned places. The liberalism of Wells and Shaw long ago lost its ascendency, and indeed in its later developments it showed what could never in the early days have been foreseen, an actual affinity with certain elements of Kipling's own constellation of ideas. And now when, in the essay which serves as the introduction to his selection of Kipling's verse, Mr. Eliot speaks of "the fascination of exploring a mind so different from my own," we surprise ourselves—as perhaps Mr. Eliot intended that we should—by seeing that the similarities between the two minds are no less striking than the differences. Time surely has done its usual but always dramatic work of eroding our clear notions of cultural antagonisms when Kipling can be thought of as in any way akin to Eliot. Yet as Mr. Eliot speaks of the public intention and the music-hall tradition of Kipling's verse, anyone who has heard a record of Mr. Eliot reading *The Waste Land* will be struck by how much that poem is publicly intended, shaped less for the study than for the platform or the pulpit, by how much the full dialect rendition of the Cockney passages suggests that it was even shaped for the music hall, by how explicit the poet's use of his voice makes the music we are so likely to think of as internal and secretive. Then it is significant that among the dominant themes of both Kipling and Eliot are those of despair and the fear of nameless psychological horror. Politically they share an excessive reliance on administration and authority. They have the same sense of being beset and betrayed by the ignoble mob; Kipling invented and elaborated the image of the Pict, the dark little hating man, "too little to love or to hate," who, if left alone, "can drag down the state"; and this figure plays its well-known part in Mr. Eliot's poetry, being for both poets the stimulus to the pathos of xenophobia.

Mr. Eliot's literary apologia for Kipling consists of asking us to judge him not as a deficient writer of poetry but as an admirable writer of verse. Upon this there follow definitions of a certain ingenuity, but the distinction between poetry and verse does not really advance beyond the old inadequate one—I believe that Mr. Eliot himself has specifically rejected it—which Matthew Arnold put forward in writing about Dryden and Pope. I cannot see the usefulness of the distinction; I can even see critical danger in it; and when Mr. Eliot says that Kipling's verse sometimes becomes poetry, it seems to me that verse, in Mr. Eliot's present sense, is merely a word used to denote poetry of a particular kind, in which certain intensities are rather low. Nowadays, it is true, we are not enough aware of the pleasures of poetry of low intensity, by which, in our modern way, we are likely to mean poetry in which the processes of thought are not, by means of elliptical or tangential metaphor and an indirect syntax, advertised as being under high pressure, Crabbe, Cowper, and Scott are rejected because they are not Donne or Hopkins or Mr. Eliot himself, or even poets of far less consequence than these; and no doubt Chaucer would be depreciated on the same grounds, if we were at all aware of him these days. I should have welcomed Mr. Eliot's speaking out in a general way in support of the admirable, and, as I think, necessary, tradition of poetry of low intensity. But by making it different in kind from poetry of high intensity and by giving it a particular name which can only be of invidious import, he has cut us off still more sharply from its virtues.

Kipling, then, must be taken as a poet. Taken so, he will scarcely rank very high, although much must be said in his praise. In two evenings, or even in a single very long one, you can read through the bulky Inclusive Edition of his verse, on which Mr. Eliot's selection is based, and be neither wearied, in part because you will not have been involved, nor uninterested, because Kipling was a man of great gifts. You will have moments of admiration, sometimes of unwilling admiration, and even wish that Mr. Eliot had included certain poems in his selection that he has left out. You will be frequently irritated by the truculence and sometimes amused by its unconsciousness —who but Kipling would write a brag about English understatement? Carlyle roaring the virtues of Silence is nothing to it—but when you have done you will be less inclined to condemn than to pity: the constant iteration of the bravado will have been illuminated by a few poems that touch on the fear and horror which Mr. Wilson speaks of at length and which Mr. Eliot refers to; you feel that the walls of wrath and the ramparts of empire are being erected against the mind's threat to itself. This is a real thing, whether we call it good or bad, and its force of reality seems to grow rather than diminish in memory, seems to be greater after one's actual reading is behind one; the quality of this reality is that which we assign to primitive and elemental things, and, judge it as we will, we dare not be indifferent or superior to it.

In speaking of Kipling's politics, Mr. Eliot contents himself with denying that Kipling was a fascist; a tory, he says, is a very different thing, a tory considers fascism the last debasement of democracy. But this, I think, is not quite ingenuous of Mr. Eliot. A tory, to be sure, is not a fascist, and Kipling is not properly to be called a fascist, but neither is his political temperament to be adequately described merely by reference to a tradition which is honored by Dr. Johnson, Burke, and Walter Scott. Kipling is not like these men; he is not generous, and, although he makes much to-do about manliness, he is not manly; and he has none of the *mind* of the few great tories. His toryism often had in it a lower-middle-class snarl of defeated gentility, and it is this, rather than his love of authority and force, that might suggest an affinity with facism. His imperialism is reprehensible not because it *is* imperialism but because it is a puny and mindless imperialism. In short, Kipling is unloved and unlovable not by reason of his beliefs but by reason of the temperament that gave them literary expression.

I have said that the old antagonism between liberalism and Kipling is now abated by time and events, yet it is still worth saying, and it is not extravagant to say, that Kipling was one of liberalism's major intellectual misfortunes. John Stuart Mill, when he urged all liberals to study the conservative Coleridge, said that we should pray to have enemies who make us worthy of ourselves. Kipling was an enemy who had the opposite effect. He tempted liberals to be content with easy victories of right feeling and with moral self-congratulation. For example, the strength of toryism at its best lies in its descent from a solid administrative tradition, while the weakness of liberalism, arising from its history of reliance upon legislation, is likely to be a fogginess about administration (or, when the fog clears away a little, a fancy and absolute notion of administration such as Wells and Shaw gave way to). Kipling's sympathy was always with the administrator and he is always suspicious of the legislator. This is foolish, but it is not the most reprehensible error in the world, and it is a prejudice which, in the hands of an intelligent man, say a man like Walter Bagehot or like Fitzjames Stephen, might make clear to the man of principled theory, to the liberal, what the difficulties not merely of government but of *governing* really are. And that is what Kipling set out to do, but he so charged his demonstration with hatred and contempt, with rancor and caste feeling, he so emptied the honorable tory tradition of its intellectual content, that he simply could not be listened to or believed, he could only be reacted against. His extravagance sprang from his hatred of the liberal intellectual—he was, we must remember, the aggressor in the quarrel —and the liberal intellectual responded by hating everything that Kipling loved, even when it had its element of virtue and enlightenment.

We must make no mistake about it—Kipling was an honest man and he loved the national virtues. But I suppose no man ever did more harm to the national virtues than Kipling did. He mixed them up with a swagger and swank, with bullying, ruthlessness, and self-righteousness, and he set them up as necessarily antagonistic to intellect. He made them stink in the nostrils of youth. I remember that in my own undergraduate days we used specifically to exclude physical courage from among the virtues; we were exaggerating the point of a joke of Shaw's and reacting from Kipling. And up to the War I had a yearly struggle with undergraduates over Wordsworth's poem, "The Character of the Happy Warrior," which is, I suppose, the respectable father of the profligate "If." [1] It seemed too moral and "manly," the students said, and once when I remarked that John Wordsworth had apparently been just such a man as his brother had described, and told them about his dutiful and courageous death at sea, they said flatly that they were not impressed. This was not what most of them really thought, but the idea of courage and duty had been steeped for them in the Kipling vat and they rejected the idea with the color. In England this response seems to have gone even further.[2] And when the War came, the interesting and touching phenomenon of the cult of Richard Hillary, which Arthur Koestler has described, was the effort of the English young men to find the national virtues without the Kipling color, to know and resist their enemies without self-glorification.

In our day the idea of the nation has become doubtful and debilitated all over the world, or at least wherever it is not being enforced by ruthless governments or wherever it is not being nourished by immediate danger or the tyranny of other nations. Men more and more think it best to postulate their loyalty either to their class, or to the idea of a social organisation more comprehensive than that of the nation, or to a cultural ideal or a spiritual fatherland. Yet in the attack which has been made on the national idea, there are, one suspects, certain motives that are not expressed, motives that have less to do with reason and order than with the modern impulse to say that politics is not really a proper human activity at all; the reluctance to give loyalty to any social organization which falls short of some ideal organisation of the future may imply a disgust not so much with the merely national life as with civic life itself. And on the posi-

1 The War over, the struggle is on again.
2 George Orwell's essay on Kipling deals bluntly and fairly with the implications of easy "liberal" and "aesthetic" contempt for *everything* Kipling stood for.

tive side too something is still to be said for nations; the case against them is not yet closed. Of course in literature nothing ever is said; every avowal of national pride or love or faith rings false and serves but to reinforce the tendency of rejection, as the example of the response to Kipling shows. Yet Kipling himself, on one occasion, dealt successfully with the national theme and in doing so implied the reason for the general failure—the "Recessional" hymn is a remarkable and perhaps a great national poem; its import of humility and fear at the moment of national success suggests that the idea of the nation, although no doubt a limited one, is still profound enough to require that it be treated with a certain measure of seriousness and truth-telling. But the occasion is exceptional with Kipling, who by the utterances that are characteristic of him did more than any writer of our time to bring the national idea into discredit.

C. S. Lewis

Kipling's World *

KIPLING is intensely loved and hated. Hardly any reader likes him a little. Those who admire him will defend him tooth and nail, and resent unfavourable criticism of him as if he were a mistress or a country rather than a writer. The other side reject him with something like personal hatred. The reason is not hard to find and will, I hope, become apparent as we go on. For the moment, I will only say that my sole qualification, if it *is* a qualification, for talking about him is that I do not fully belong to either side.

I have been reading him off and on all my life, and I never return to him without renewed admiration. I have never at any time been able to understand how a man of taste could doubt that Kipling is a very great artist. On the other hand, I have never quite taken him to my heart. He is not one of my indispensables; life would go on much the same if the last copy of his works disappeared. I can go even further than this. Not only is my allegiance imperfect, it is also inconstant. After I have been reading Kipling for some days together there comes a sudden check. One moment I am filled with delight at the variety and solidity of his imagination; and then, the very next moment, I am sick, sick to death, of the whole Kipling world. Of course, one can reach temporary saturation point with any

* [From *They Asked for a Paper* (London, 1963). Delivered as a lecture in 1948 and reprinted in *The Kipling Journal*, XXV, Nos. 127, 128 (Sept., Dec., 1958), 8–16, 7–11. Reprinted by permission of Geoffrey Bles, Ltd.]

author; there comes an evening when even Boswell or Virgil will do no longer. But one parts from them as a friend: one knows one will want them another day; and in the interval one thinks of them with pleasure. But I mean something quite different from that; I mean a real disenchantment, a recoil which makes the Kipling world, for the moment, not dull (it is never that), but unendurable—a heavy, glaring, suffocating monstrosity. It is the difference between feeling that, on the whole, you would not like another slice of bread and butter just now and wondering, as your gorge rises, how you could ever have imagined that you liked vodka.

I by no means assume that this sudden change of feeling is reasonable. But it must certainly have causes, and I hope that to explore them may cast some light on Kipling. I am going to suggest that they are two in number, one arising from what may be called the formal, the other from what may be called the material, character of his work. I admit that this distinction of form from matter breaks down if you press it too far or in certain directions, but I think it will do for the purpose I have in hand.

The first cause for my sudden recoil from Kipling I take to be not the defect but the excess of his art. He himself has told us how he licked every story into its final shape. He dipped a brush in Indian ink and then re-read the manuscript "in an auspicious hour," considering faithfully "every paragraph, sentence and word" and "blacking out where requisite." After a time he re-read the story and usually found that it would bear "a second shortening." Finally there came a third reading, at which still more deletion might or might not be found necessary. It is a magnificent example of self-discipline, which Horace would have approved. But I suggest that even an athlete can be over-trained. Superfluous flesh should be sweated off; but a cruel trainer may be too severe in judging what is superfluous. I think Kipling used the Indian ink too much. Sometimes the story has been so compressed that in the completed version it is not quite told—at least, I still do not know exactly what happened in *Mrs. Bathurst*. But even when this is not so, the art over-reaches itself in another way. Every sentence that did not seem to Kipling perfectly and triumphantly good has been removed.

As a result, the style tends to be too continuously and obtrusively brilliant. The result is a little fatiguing. Our author gives us no rest: we are bombarded with felicities till they deafen us. There is no elbow room, no leisureliness. We need roughage as well as nourishment in a diet; but there is no roughage in a Kipling story—it is all unrelieved vitamins from the first word to the last.

To this criticism I think Kipling could make an almost perfectly satisfactory answer. He might say that he was writing short stories and short poems, each of which was to be the only specimen of Kipling in some number of a periodical. His work was meant to be taken in small doses. The man who gobbles down one story after another at a sitting has no more right to complain if the result is disastrous than the man who swills liqueurs as if they were beer. This answer, I have said, seems to me almost complete. Almost—because even inside a single story the brilliance of the parts, in my opinion, sometimes damages the effect of the whole. I am thinking of *My Sunday at Home*. The fancied situation is excellent; one ought to remember the story with chuckles as one remembers *The Wrong Box*. But I know I am not alone in finding that one actually laughed less than one would have thought possible in the reading of it and that in remembering it one always reverts to the summer drowsiness of the Wiltshire country around the railway station. That superb piece of scene painting has almost blotted out the comic action. Yet I suppose it was originally introduced for no other purpose than to emphasize the solitude of the place.

The fault of which I am here accusing Kipling is one which only a great artist could commit. For most of us the old rule of cutting out every word that can be spared is still a safe one: there is no danger that even after this process the result will be too vivid and too full of sense. And, as far as mere art is concerned, I think this almost the only fault I can find in Kipling's mature work; I say his mature work for, of course, like all men, he made some unsuccessful experiments before he found his true vein. It is when I turn to his matter that my serious discontents begin.

The earliest generation of Kipling's readers regarded him as the mouthpiece of patriotism and imperialism. I think that conception of his work is inadequate. Chesterton did a great service to criticism by contradicting it in a famous chapter of *Heretics*. In that chapter he finds the essential characteristics of Kipling's mind to be two. In the first place he had discovered, or rediscovered, the poetry of common things; had perceived, as Chesterton says, "the significance and philosophy of steam and of slang." In the second place, Kipling was the poet of discipline. Not specially, nor exclusively, of military discipline, but of discipline in every shape. "He has not written so well of soldiers," says Chesterton, "as he has of railwaymen or bridgebuilders, or even journalists." This particular judgment may be disputed, but I feel no doubt at all that Chesterton has picked up the right scent.

To put the thing in the shortest possible way, Kipling is first and foremost the poet of work. It is really remarkable how poetry and fiction before his time had avoided this subject. They had dealt almost exclusively with men in their "private hours"— with love affairs, crimes, sport, illness, and changes of fortune. Mr. Osborne may be a merchant, but *Vanity Fair* has no interest in his mercantile life. Darcy was a good landlord and Wentworth a good officer, but their activities in these capacities are all "off stage." Most of Scott's characters, except the soldiers, have no profession; and when they are soldiers the emphasis is on battles and adventures, not on the professional routine. Business comes into Dickens only in so far as it is criminal or comic. With a few exceptions, imaginative literature in the eighteenth and nineteenth centuries had quietly omitted, or at least thrust into the background, the sort of thing which, in fact, occupies most of the waking hours of most men. And this did not merely mean that certain technical aspects of life were unrepresented. A whole range of strong sentiments and emotions —for many men, the strongest of all—went with them. For, as Pepys once noted with surprise, there is great pleasure in talking of business. It was Kipling who first reclaimed for literature this enormous territory.

His early stories of Anglo-Indian society still conform to the older convention. They are about love affairs, elopements, intrigues, and domestic quarrels. They are indeed connected with his later and more characteristic work by a thread which I shall discuss presently; but on the surface they are a different kind of thing. The *Departmental Ditties* are much more typical of the author's real interests. The point about Potiphar Gubbins is not simply that he is a cuckold but that his horns bring him advancement in the Civil Service and that he builds very bad bridges. The sting of *The Story of Uriah* lies not merely in the wife's depravity but in the fact that the husband was sent, for her lover's convenience, to die at Quetta, "attempting two men's duty in that very healthy post." Exeter Battleby Tring, who really knows something about railways, has his mouth silenced with rupees in order that "the Little Tin Gods (long may their Highnesses thrive!)" may keep "their Circle intact." Boanerges Blitzen ruins his official career by exposing "office scandals" in the papers. The whole bitter little collection presents a corrupt society, not in its leisure, but in its official corruption. In his later work this preference for depicting men at their jobs becomes his most obvious characteristic. Findlayson's hopes and fears about his bridge, McPhee's attitude both to engines and owners, William the Conqueror's work in the famine district, a lighthousekeeper at his post on a foggy night, Gisborne and his chief in the forest, McAndrew standing his watch—these are the things that come back to us when we remember Kipling; and there had really been nothing like them in literature before. The poems again and again strike the same note. Lord Dufferin (heavily influenced by Bishop Blougram) hands on the *arcana imperii* to Lord Lansdowne; the professional spies set out, "each man reporting for duty alone, out of sight, out of reach of his fellow"; the crew of the *Bolivar*, "mad with work and weariness," see "some damned Liner's lights go by like a grand hotel"; H. Mukerji ends with the Boh's head a covering letter in perfect Babu officialese; the fans and beltings in a munition factory roar round a widowed war worker. The rhythms of work—boots slogging along a road, the Harrild and the Hoe devouring "their league-long paper-bale," the grunting of a water-wheel—echo through Kipling's verse and prose as through no other man's. Even Mowgli in the end accepts a post in the Civil Service. Even *The Brushwood Boy* turns aside from its main theme to show how much toil its hero suffered and inflicted in the course of his professional career. Even when

we are taken into the remote past, Kipling is not interested in
imagining what it felt like to be an ancient and pagan man;
only in what it felt like to be a man doing some ancient job—
a galley slave, a Roman officer. How the light came in through
the oar-holes in the galley—that little detail which everyone who
had served in a galley would remember and which no one else
would know—that is Kipling's quarry.

It would be quite a mistake, however, to accuse Kipling of
swamping the human interest in his mass of material and technical detail. The detail is there for the sake of a human interest,
but that human interest is one that no previous writer had
done justice to. What Kipling chiefly communicates—and it is,
for good and for ill, one of the strongest things in the world—
is the peculiar relation which men who do the same work have
to that work and to one another; the inescapable bond of
shared experiences, and, above all, of shared hardships. It is
a commitment for life:

> Oh, was there ever sailor free to choose,
>   That didn't settle somewhere near the sea?
> We've only one virginity to lose,
>   And where we lost it, there our hearts will be!

That is why in *Steam Tactics* Hinchcliffe, who, when starting
on his leave, had "thanked his Maker that he wouldn't see nor
smell nor thumb a runnin' bulgine till the nineteenth prox,"
nevertheless fell immediately to studying the engine of Kipling's
steam-car.

For the same reason, Kipling, the old journalist, writes:

> But the Jew shall forget Jerusalem
>   Ere we forget the Press.

In the next stanza he goes on to explain why. The man who
has "stood through the loaded hour" and "lit his pipe in the
morning calm"—who has, in fact, been through the nocturnal
routine of producing a newspaper—"hath sold his heart." That
is the whole point. We who are of one trade (whether journalists, soldiers, galley slaves, Indian Civilians, or what you will)
know so many things that the outsiders will never, never understand. Like the two child lovers in *The Light that Failed*, "we

belong." It is a bond which in real life sometimes proves stronger than any other:

> The men of my own stock
> They may do ill or well,
> But they tell the lies I am wonted to,
> They are used to the lies I tell;
> And we do not need interpreters
> When we go to buy and sell.

How true to life is the immediate alliance of the three journalists whom chance has thrown together in the story called *A Matter of Fact*.

This spirit of the profession is everywhere shown in Kipling as a ruthless master. That is why Chesterton got in a very large part of the truth when he fixed on discipline as Kipling's main subject. There is nothing Kipling describes with more relish than the process whereby the trade-spirit licks some raw cub into shape. That is the whole theme of one of his few full-length novels, *Captains Courageous*. It is the theme of *The Centaurs*, and of *Pharaoh and the Sergeant*, and on *The 'Eathen*. It is allegorically expressed in *The Ship that Found Herself*. It is implicit in all the army stories and the sea stories; indeed, it may be thought that the author turns aside from his narrative rather too often to assure us that Mulvaney was invaluable for "licking the new batch of recruits into shape." Even when we escape into the jungle and the wolf pack we do not escape the Law. Until he has been disciplined—"put through it," licked into shape—a man is, for Kipling, mere raw material. "Gad," says Hitchcock to Findlayson in *The Bridge-Builders*, "what a Cooper's Hill cub I was when I came on the works." And Findlayson muses, "Cub thou wast; assistant thou art." The philosophy of the thing is summed up at the end of *A Walking Delegate*, where the yellow horse (an agitator) has asked the old working horse, "Have you no respec' whatever for the dignity o' our common horsehood?" He gets the reply, "Horse, sonny, is what you start from. We know all about horse here, an' he ain't any high-toned, pure-souled child of nature. Horse, plain horse, same ez you, is chock-full o' tricks an' meannesses an' cussednesses an' monkey shines. . . . That's horse, an' thet's about his dignity an' the size of his soul 'fore he's been broke an' raw-hided a piece." Reading "man" for "horse," we here have Kipling's doctrine of Man.

This is one of the most important things Kipling has to say and one which he means very seriously, and it is also one of the things which has aroused hatred against him. It amounts to something like a doctrine of original sin, and it is antipathetic to many modern modes of thought. Perhaps even more anti-pathetic is Kipling's presentation of the "breaking" and "raw hiding" process. In *His Private Honour* it turns out to consist of prolonged bullying and incessant abuse; the sort of bullying (as we learn from *The 'Eathen*) which sends grown men off to cry in solitude, followed by the jeers of the old hands. The pa-tient is not allowed to claim any personal rights whatever; there is nothing, according to Kipling, more subversive. To ask for justice is as the sin of witchcraft. The disaster in the poem called *That Day* began with the fact that "every little drummer 'ad 'is rights an' wrongs to mind." In contrast, "My rights," Ortheris answered with deep scorn, "my rights! I ain't a recruity to go whinin' about my rights to this an' my rights to that, just as if I couldn't look after myself. My rights! 'Strewth A'mighty! I'm a man."

Now there is no good whatever in dismissing this part of Kipling's message as if it were not worth powder and shot. There is a truth in it which must be faced before we attempt to find any larger truths which it may exclude. Many who hate Kipling have omitted this preliminary. They feel instinctively that they themselves are just the unlicked or unbroken men whom Kipling condemns; they find the picture intolerable, and the picture of the cure more intolerable still. To escape, they dismiss the whole thing as a mere fascist or "public school" brutality. But there is no solution along those lines. It may (or may not) be possible to get beyond Kipling's harsh wisdom; but there is no getting beyond a thing without first getting as far. It is a brutal truth about the world that the whole everlasting business of keeping the human race protected and clothed and fed could not go on for twenty-four hours without the vast legion of hard-bitten, technically efficient, not-over-sympathetic men, and with-out the harsh processes of discipline by which this legion is

made. It is a brutal truth that unless a great many people practised the Kipling *ethos* there would be neither security nor
leisure for any people to practise a finer *ethos*. As Chesterton
admits, "We may fling ourselves into a hammock in a fit of
divine carelessness; but we are glad that the maker did not
make the hammock in a fit of divine carelessness." In *The
Proconsuls*, speaking of those who have actually ruled with a
strong hand, Kipling says:

> On the stage their act hath framed
>   For thy sports, O Liberty!
> Doubted are they, and defamed
>   By the tongues their act set free.

It is a true bill, as far as it goes. Unless the Kipling virtues—
if you will, the Kipling vices—had long and widely been practised in the world we should be in no case to sit here and discuss
Kipling. If all men stood talking of their rights before they
went up a mast or down a sewer or stoked a furnace or joined
an army, we should all perish; nor while they talked of their
rights would they learn to do these things. And I think we must
agree with Kipling that the man preoccupied with his own rights
is not only a disastrous, but a very unlovely object; indeed, one
of the worst mischiefs we do by treating a man unjustly is that
we force him to be thus preoccupied.

But if so, then it is all the more important that men should,
in fact, be treated with justice. If we all need "licking into
shape" and if, while undergoing the process, we must not guard
our rights, then it is all the more important that someone else
should guard them for us. What has Kipling to say on this subject? For, quite clearly, the very same methods which he pre-
scribes for licking the cub into shape, "making a man of him"
in the interests of the community, would also, if his masters
were bad men, be an admirable method of keeping the cub
quiet while he was exploited and enslaved for their private
benefit. It is all very well that the colts (in *The Centaurs*)
should learn to obey Chiron as a means to becoming good
cavalry chargers; but how if Chiron wants their obedience only
to bring them to the knacker's yard? And are the masters never
bad men? From some stories one would almost conclude that

Kipling is ignorant of, or indifferent to, this possibility. In *His Private Honour* the old soldiers educate the recruits by continued bullying. But Kipling seems quite unaware that bullying is an activity which human beings *enjoy*. We are given to understand that the old soldiers are wholly immune to this temptation; they threaten, mock, and thrash the recruits only from the highest possible motives. Is this naïvety in the author? Can he really be so ignorant? Or does he not care?

He is certainly not ignorant. Most of us begin by regarding Kipling as the panegyrist of the whole imperial system. But we find, when we look into the matter, that his admiration is reserved for those in the lower positions. These are the "men on the spot"; the bearers of the burden; above them we find folly and ignorance; at the centre of the whole thing we find the terrible society of Simla, a provincial smart set which plays frivolously with men's careers and even their lives. The system is rotten at the head, and official advancement may have a *teterrima causa*. Findlayson had to see "months of office work destroyed at a blow when the Government of India at the last moment added two feet to the width of the bridge under the impression that bridges were cut out of paper!" The heart-rending death of Orde (one of Kipling's best tragic scenes) is followed by the undoing of his life's work when the ignorant Viceroy sends a Babu to succeed him. In *Tods' Amendment* disaster is averted by a child who knows what all the rulers of India (the "little Tin Gods") do not know. It is interesting to compare *The 'Eathen* with *The Sergeant's Wedding*. In the one, the sergeants are benevolent despots—it is only the softness and selfishness of the recruit that make them think they are cruel tyrants. In the other, we have a sergeant who uses his position to make money by cheating the men. Clearly this sergeant would have just as strong a motive as the good ones for detesting privates who talked about their "rights and wrongs."

All this suggests that the disciplinary system is a very two-edged affair; but this does not in the least shake Kipling's devotion to it. That, he says in effect, is what the world always has been like and always will be like. Even in prehistoric times the astute person

> Won a simple Viceroy's praise
> Through the toil of other men.

And no one can rebuke more stunningly than Kipling those who exploit and frustrate the much-enduring "man on the spot":

> When the last grim joke is entered
> In the big black Book of jobs,
> And Quetta graveyards give again
> Their victims to the air,
> I shouldn't like to be the man
> Who sent Jack Barrett there.

But this makes no difference to the duty of the sufferer. Whatever corruptions there may be at the top, the work must go on; frontiers must be protected, epidemics fought, bridges built, marshes drained, famine relief administered. Protest, however well-grounded, about injustice, and schemes of reform, will never bring a ship into harbour or a train into the station or sow a field of oats or quell a riot; and "the unforgiving minute" is upon us fourteen hundred and forty times a day. This is the truest and finest element in Kipling; his version of Carlyle's gospel of work. It has affinities with Piers Plowman's insistence on ploughing his half-acre; but there are important differences.

The more Kipling convinces us that no plea for justice or happiness must be allowed to interfere with the job, the more anxious we become for reassurance that the work is really worthy of all the human sacrifices it demands. "The game," he says, "is more than the player of the game." But perhaps some games are and some aren't. "And the ship is more than the crew"— but one would like to know where the ship was going and why. Was its voyage really useful—or even innocent? We want, in fact, a doctrine of Ends. Langland could supply one. He knows how Do Well is connected with Do Better and Do Best; the ploughing of the half-acre is placed in a cosmic context and that context would enable Langland, in principle, to tell us whether any given job in the whole universe was true worship or miserable idolatry; it is here that Kipling speaks with an uncertain voice. For many of the things done by his Civil Servants the necessity is perhaps obvious; but that is not a side of the matter he develops. And he writes with equal relish where the ultimate ends of the work described are much less

obvious. Sometimes his choice of sides seems to be quite accidental, even frivolous. When William the Conqueror met a
schoolmaster who had to teach the natives the beauties of
Wordsworth's *Excursion,* she told him rather unnecessarily, "I
like men who do things." Teaching English Literature to natives
is not "doing things," and we are meant to despise that schoolmaster. One notes that the editor of the local paper, whom we
met a few pages before, is visited with no similar ignominy. Yet
it is easy enough to imagine the situations reversed. Kipling
could have written a perfect Kipling story about two men in
the Educational Department working eighteen hours a day to
conduct an examination, with punkah flapping and all the usual
background. The futility of the curriculum which makes them
set Wordsworth to Indian schoolboys would not in the least
have detracted from their heroism if he had chosen to write the
story from that point of view. It would have been their professional grievance—ironically and stoically endured—one more
instance of that irresponsible folly at the top which wastes and
breaks the men who really do the work. I have a disquieting
feeling that Kipling's actual respect for the journalist and contempt for the schoolmaster has no thought-out doctrine of ends
behind it, but results from the accident that he himself worked
for a newspaper and not for a school. And now, at last, I begin
to suspect that we are finding a clue to that suffocating sensation which overtakes me if I read Kipling too long. Is the Kipling
world really monstrous in the sense of being misshaped? How
if this doctrine of work and discipline, which is so clear and
earnest and dogmatic at the periphery, hides at the centre a
terrible vagueness, a frivolity or scepticism?

Sometimes it hides nothing but what the English, whether
fairly or unfairly, are inclined to call Americanism. The story
called *Below the Mill Dam* is an instance. We are expected to
rejoice that the native black rat should be superseded by the
alien brown rat; that the mill wheel could be yoked to a dynamo
and the countryside electrified. None of the questions which
every thinking man must raise about the beneficence of this
whole transition have any meaning for Kipling. They are to
him mere excuses for idleness. "We have already learned six
refined synonyms for loafing," say the waters; and, to the Wheel

itself, "While you're at work you'll work." The black rat is to be
stuffed. Here is the creed of Activism—of "Progress," hustle, and
development—all blind, naked, uncritical of itself. Similarly
in *The Explorer,* while we admire the man's courage in the
earlier stanzas, the end which he has in view gives us pause.
His Holy Grail is simply the industrialization of the country he
has discovered. The waterfalls are "wasting fifty thousand head
an hour" and the forests are "axe-ripe"; he will rectify this. The
End, here as in the Mill Dam story, may be a good one; it is
not for me to decide. But Kipling does not seem to know there
is any question. In *Bread upon the Waters* all the usual hardships are described and with all Kipling's usual relish; but the
only end is money and revenge—though, I confess, a very ex-
cusable revenge. In *The Devil and the Deep Sea* the job, which
is treated with his usual reverence, the game, which is still more
than the player of the game, is merely the triumph of a gang
of criminals.

This might be explained by saying that Kipling is not a
moralist but a purely objective writer. But that would be false.
He is eminently a moralist; in almost every story we are invited,
nay forced, to admire and condemn. Many of the poems are
versified homilies. That is why this chanciness or uncertainty
about the end to which the moralism of his *bushido* is applied
in any particular instance makes us uncomfortable. And now
we must take a step further. Even Discipline is not a constant.
The very people who would be cubs to be licked into shape in
one story may, in another, be the heroes we are asked to admire.

Stalky and his friends are inveterate breakers of discipline.
How easily, had his own early memories been different, could
Kipling have written the story the other way round. In *Their
Lawful Occasions* Moorshed, because he is rich and able to leave
the Navy next year, can afford to take an independent line.
All Kipling's sympathy is with him and against the ship which
is significantly named H.M.S. *Pedantic.* Yet Kipling need only
have altered the lighting (so to speak) to make Moorshed, and
the grounds of his independence, particularly odious and the
odium would have been of a characteristically Kiplingese kind.
In *Without Benefit of Clergy* Holden's inefficiency as a civil
servant is made light of; but had Kipling written in a different

mood the very cause of this inefficiency—namely, keeping a native mistress—would have been made into a despicable aggravation. In the actual story it is almost an excuse. In *The Germ Destroyer* we actually find Kipling laughing at a man because he has "a marked passion for work!" In *The Bisara of Pooree* that whole Anglo-Indian world, whose work for the natives elsewhere seems so necessary and valuable, is contrasted with the natives as "the shiny, top-scum stuff that people call civilization." In *The Dream of Duncan Parrenness*, the apparition offers the hero success in the Anglo-Indian career in return for his Trust in Man, his Faith in Woman, and his Boy's Conscience. He gives them all and receives in return "a little piece of dry bread." Where now is the Kipling we thought we knew—the prophet of work, the activist, the writer of *If*? "Were it not better done as others use . . . ?"

You may say that some of these examples are taken from early stories; perhaps Kipling held these sceptical views in his youth and abandoned them in his maturity. Perhaps—as I once half-believed myself—he is a "lost leader"; a great opposition writer who was somehow caught by government. I think there was a change in his views, but I do not think that goes to the root of the matter. I think that nearly all his work (for there are a few, and very valuable, exceptions) at all periods is dominated by one master passion. What he loves better than anything in the world is the intimacy within a closed circle—even if it be only a circle of shared misery as in *Helen All Alone* or of shared crime as in *The Devil and the Deep Sea*. In the last resort I do not think he loves professional brotherhood for the sake of work; I think he loves work for the sake of professional brotherhood. Out of that passion all his apparently contradictory moods arise. But I must attempt to define the passion itself a little more closely and to show how it has such a diversified offspring.

When we foregather with three or four trusted cronies of our own calling, a strong sense of community arises and is enjoyed. But that enjoyment can be prolonged by several different kinds of conversation. We may all be engaged in standing together against the outer world—all those fools outside who write newspaper articles about us which reveal their ghastly ignorance of the real work, and propose schemes which look very fine on paper but which, as we well know, are impracticable. As long as that conversation lasts, the profession appears a very fine one and its achievements very remarkable; if only those yapping outsiders would leave us alone to get on with the job. And that conversation, if we could do it well enough, would make *one* kind of Kipling story. But we might equally spend the evening standing together against our own seniors: those people at the top—Lord knows how they got there while better men rot in provincial lectureships, or small ships, or starving parishes!—who seem to have forgotten what the real work is like and who spoil all our best efforts with their meddling and are quite deceived about our relative merits. And while that conversation lasted, our profession would appear a very rotten and heart-breaking profession. We might even say it was high time the public learned the sort of things that really go on. A rousing scandal might do good. And out of all that *another* Kipling story might be made. But then, some other evening, or later the same evening, we might all be standing together against our juniors. As if by magic our profession would now once more appear in a favourable light—at least, our profession as it used to be. What may happen with the sort of young cubs we're getting into it nowadays is another question. They need licking into shape. They'll have to learn to pull their socks up. They haven't begun to realise what is expected of them. And heaven knows, things are made easy enough for them now! They haven't been through the sort of mill we went through. God! It they'd worked under old So-and-so . . . and thus, yet *another* Kipling story might arise. But we sometimes like talking about our juniors in exactly the opposite way. We have been in the job so long that we have no illusions about it. We know that half the official regulations are dead letters. Nobody will thank you for doing more than you need. Our juniors are laughably full of zeal, pedantic about discipline, devoured with a morbid passion for work. Ah, well, they'll soon get over it!

Now the point is that the similarity between all these conversations is overwhelmingly more important than the differences. It may well be mere chance which launches the evening on one of them rather than another, for they all give the same kind of pleasure, and that is the kind of pleasure which the great majority of Kipling's works both express and communicate. I am tempted to describe it as the pleasure of freemasonry; but this would be confusing because Kipling became a Mason in the narrower and official sense. But in the wider sense you may say he was born a Mason. One of the stories that pleased his childhood was, significantly, about "lions who were all Freemasons" and in "confederacy against some wicked baboons." The pleasure of confederacy against wicked baboons, or even of confederacy *simpliciter*, is the cardinal fact about the Kipling world. To belong, to be inside, to be in the know, to be snugly together against the outsiders—that is what really matters; it is almost an accident who are cast for the rôle of outsiders (wicked baboons) on any given occasion. And no one before Kipling had fully celebrated the potency of that snugness—the esoteric comedies and tragedies, the mutual understanding, the highly specialised smile, or shrug, or nod, or shake of the head which passes between fellow-professionals; the exquisite pleasure of being approved, the unassuaged mortification of being despised, within that charmed circle, compared with which public fame and infamy are a mere idle breath. What is the good of "the papers hiding it proper" if "you know the army knows?" What is the good of excuses accepted by the government if "the men of one's own kind" hold one condemned?

And this is how the Simla stories really fit in. They are not very good—Kipling's women all have baritone voices—and at first sight they are not very mature work. But look again. "If you don't know about things Up Above," says Kipling, after recording one of Mrs. Hauksbee's most improbable exploits, "you won't understand how to fit in, and you will say it is impossible." In other words, at this stage of Kipling's career Simla society (to which, it may be supposed, his *entrée* was rather precarious) is itself a secret society, an inner ring, and the stories about it are for those who are "in the know." That the secrets in this case should be very shabby ones and the knowledge offered is very disillusioned knowledge, is an effect of the writer's youth. Young writers, and especially young writers already enchanted by the lure of the Inner Ring, like to exaggerate the cynicism and sophistication of the great world; it

makes them feel less young. One sees how he must have enjoyed writing "Simla is a strange place . . . nor is any man
who has not spent at least ten seasons there qualified to pass
judgment!" That is the spirit of nearly all Kipling's work,
though it was later applied to inner rings more interesting than
Simla. There is something delicious about these early flights of
esotericism. "In India," he says, "where everyone knows everyone else"; and again "I have lived long enough in India to know
nothing."

The great merit of Kipling is to have presented the magic of
the Inner Ring in all its manifold workings for the first time.
Earlier writers had presented it only in the form of snobbery;
and snobbery is a very highly specialised form of it. The call of
the Inner Ring, the men we know, the old firm, the talking of
"shop," may call a man away from high society into very low
society indeed; we desire not to be in a *junto* simply, just to be
in that *junto* where we "belong." Nor is Kipling in the least
mistaken when he attributes to this esoteric spirit such great
powers for good. The professional point of honour (it means as
much, said McPhee, as her virginity to a lassie), the *Aidôs* which
we feel only before our colleagues, the firm brotherhood of
those who have "been through it" together, are things quite
indispensable to the running of the world. This masonry or
confederacy daily carries commonplace people to heights of
diligence or courage which they would not be likely to reach
by any private moral ideals. Without it, no good thing is operative widely or for long.

But also—and this Kipling never seems to notice—without
it no bad thing is operative either. The nostalgia which sends
the old soldier back to the army ("I smelled the smell of the
barracks, I 'eard the bugles go") also sends the recidivist back
to his old partner and his old 'fence.' The confidential glance
or rebuke from a colleague is indeed the means whereby a weak
brother is brought or kept up to the standard of a noble profession; it is also the means whereby a new and hitherto innocent member is initiated into the corruption of a bad one. "It's
always done," they say; and so, without any 'scenes' or excite-
ment, with a nod and a wink, over a couple of whiskies and
soda, the Rubicon is crossed. The spirit of the Inner Ring is

morally neutral—the obedient servant of valour and public spirit, but equally of cruelty, extortion, oppression, and dishonesty.

Kipling seems unaware of this, or indifferent to it. He is the slave of the Inner Ring; he expresses the passion, but does not stand outside to criticise it. He plays for his side; about the choice of sides, about the limitations of partnership after the side has been chosen, he has nothing very much to say to us. Mr. Eliot has, I think rightly, called him a Pagan. Irreverence is the last thing of which one could accuse him. He has a reverent Pagan agnosticism about all ultimates. "When a man has come to the turnstiles of Night," he says in the preface to *Life's Handicap*, "all the creeds in the world seem to him wonderfully alike and colourless." He has the Pagan tolerance, too; a tolerance so wide (which is unusual) that it extends even to Christianity, whose phraseology he freely uses for rhetorical effect in his more Swinburnian moments (some poems could not, on internal evidence alone, be distinguished from Christian work). But the tolerance is weary and sceptical; the whole energy of the man goes into his worship of the little demigods or dæmons in the foreground—the Traders, the Sides, the Inner Rings. Their credentials he hardly examines. These servants he has made masters; these half-gods exclude the gods.

There are, I allow, hints in his work of another Kipling. There are moments of an almost quivering tenderness—he himself had been badly hurt—when he writes of children or for them. And there are the "queer" or "rum" stories—*At the End of the Passage, The Mark of the Beast, They, Wireless*. These may be his best work, but they are not his most characteristic. If you open him at random, the chances are you will find him enslaved to some Inner Ring. His English countryside with its way of life is partly loved because American millionaires can't understand it, aren't in the know. His comic stories are nearly all about hoaxes: an outsider mystified is his favourite joke. His jungle is not free from it. His very railway engines are either recruits or Mulvaneys dressed up in boilers. His polo-ponies are public school ponies. Even his saints and angels are in a celestial civil service. Finally, something so simple and ordinary as an enjoyment of Jane Austen's novels is turned into the pretext for one more secret society, and we have the hardly forgivable *Janeites*. It is this ubiquitous presence of the Ring, this unwearied knowingness, that renders his work in the long run suffocating and unendurable. And always, ironically, that bleak misgiving—almost that Nothingness—in the background.

But he was a very great writer. This trade-passion, this business of the Inner Ring, fills an immense area of human life. There, though not in the conventional novel, it frequently proves itself stronger than family affection, national loyalty, religion, and even vice. Hence Kipling's deserved success with thousands of readers who left the older fiction to be read by women and boys. He came home to their bosoms by coming home to their business and showed them life as they had found it to be. This is merit of a high order; it is like the discovery of a new element or a new planet; it is, in its way and as far as it goes, a "return to nature." The remedy for what is partial and dangerous in his view of life is to go on from Kipling and to add the necessary correctives—not to deny what he has shown. After Kipling there is no excuse for the assumption that all the important things in a man's life happen between the end of one day's work and the beginning of the next. There is no good putting on airs about Kipling. The things he mistook for gods may have been only "spirits of another sort"; but they are real things and strong.

T. S. Eliot

The Unfading Genius of Rudyard Kipling *

WHEN I RECEIVED the invitation to propose the toast at the annual luncheon of the Kipling Society, I felt no hestitation in accepting. It came to me like a decree of Destiny: a feeling which I think Kipling himself would have understood. I am often enough invited to speak, but the feeling to which I refer comes to me very seldom. It is a very different emotion from that of the mere inescapability of a task accepted only because one can find no plausible reason for declining. Nor, I hasten to add, does it mean that I considered myself either an authority on the subject, or in the least gifted as an after-dinner speaker. It is simply that I have come to have a feeling, almost a superstition, that it is a kind of obligation laid upon me to testify for Rudyard Kipling whenever the opportunity presents itself.

Rudyard Kipling, whom I never knew and never saw, and who probably never heard of me, has touched my life at sundry times and in divers manners. In 1939, I was elected to an Honorary Fellowship of Magdalene College, Cambridge, of which the previous incumbent had been Kipling. In 1941, I was invited to prepare a selection of Kipling's verse and to provide a long introduction. Two weeks ago I was in Paris, being introduced into a society called the Académie Septentrionale, where I had to pronounce the *éloge* of my predecessor—Rudyard Kipling. And here I am today to perform a similar function.

* [From *The Kipling Journal*, XXVI, No. 129 (March, 1959), pp. 9–12. Delivered as an address in 1958. Reprinted by permission of the author.]

All this might be dismissed as coincidence, or as a series in which one event led to another. But Kipling has accompanied me ever since boyhood, when I discovered the early verse— "Barrack Room Ballads"—and the early stories—"Plain Tales from the Hills." There are boyhood enthusiasms which one outgrows; there are writers who impress one deeply at some time before or during adolescence and whose work one never re-reads in later life. But Kipling is different. Traces of Kipling appear in my own mature verse where no diligent scholarly sleuth has yet observed them, but which I am myself prepared to disclose. I once wrote a poem called "The Love Song of J. Alfred Prufrock": I am convinced that it would never have been called "Love Song" but for a title of Kipling's that stuck obstinately in my head: "The Love Song of Har Dyal." Many years later I wrote a poem called "The Hollow Men": I could never have thought of this title but for Kipling's poem "The Broken Men." One of the broken men has turned up recently in my work, and may be seen at this time on the stage of the Cambridge Theatre. And I leave you to guess why a Persian cat I once possessed was dignified by the name of Mirza Murad Ali Beg.

So much to explain to you my feeling of destiny. When I made the selection from Kipling's verse which I have already mentioned, in 1941, the moment was well chosen to remind the public of Kipling's importance, and to revive a reputation which had diminished under the influence of liberal, not to say radical critics. But it aroused considerable astonishment in the world of letters, that Kipling should be championed not only as a prose writer but as a writer of verse, by a poet whose verse was generally considered to be at the opposite pole from Kipling's. Whereas my poems had appeared too obscure and recondite to win popular approval, Kipling's had long been considered too simple, too crude, too popular, indeed too near the doggerel of the music hall song, to deserve from the fastidious critic anything but disdain. I was suspected, if not of insincerity, at least of a mischievous delight in paradox. Yet I think that the facts which I have just recounted should convince the present audience that this was not true.

There is perhaps a reason of a different order than any I

have so far implied, for my regard for Kipling's work, a reason
given by a similarity, or rather an analogy, between his background and mine. Kipling passed his early childhood in India;
he was brought back to England for his schooling; he returned
to India at the age of seventeen. Two years of his life were
spent in America. Later, he settled in Sussex, but came to pass
his winters in the more benign climate of South Africa. He had
been a citizen of the British Empire, long before he naturalised
himself, so to speak, in a particular part of a particular county
of England. The topography of my own life history is very different from his, but our feeling about England springs from
causes not wholly dissimilar. The word *metic* is perfectly good
English, though to many people the French *métèque* may be
more familiar. It does not apply perhaps in the strictest sense
to either of us, since we come both from wholly British stock;
but I think that Kipling's attitude to things English, like mine,
was in some ways different from that of any native-born Briton.
I feel this in some of the poems written after Kipling settled in
Sussex. For example, "The Recall":

> Under their feet in the grasses
> My clinging magic runs.
> They shall return as strangers,
> They shall remain as sons.

He is referring to the American couple of the story which this
poem accompanies, who settle in England in the village from
which the wife's family had gone to America: but I feel that he
is writing out of his own experience. Similarly, in "Sir Richard's
Song" the speaker is a Norman knight, a follower of William
the Conqueror, who has settled in England:

> I followed my Duke ere I was a lover,
>   To take from England fief and fee;
> But now this game is the other way over—
>   But now England hath taken me!

Sir Richard, too, I think, is Kipling himself.

What is one to say, in a few minutes, about the amazing
man of genius, every single piece of writing of whom, taken in
isolation, can look like a brilliant *tour de force*; but whose work

has nevertheless an undeniable unity? There are at least half a dozen aspects of Kipling upon which one would like to dilate: the journalist, the literary artist, the observer of men, of landscapes and countries and of machines also, the moralist, the curious seeker into the abnormal and paranormal, and the seer. To do justice to Kipling, to draw the portrait of the man in his writings, one would have to consider him under all of these aspects, and then show the unity behind them. I can touch today only upon two aspects which seem to me of special importance: those of the moralist and the seer.

The moralist in Kipling appears constantly throughout his work: it is one of the elements which contribute to make unity of it. Often, it approximates to a kind of stoicism, in the popular use of that word: the man held up for admiration is the man who has done his allotted task, without the expectation of reward or concern with recognition. Thus the "Sons of Martha":

It is their care in all the ages to take the buffet and cushion the
    shock.
It is their care that the gear engages; it is their care that the switches
    lock.
It is their care that the wheels run truly; it is their care to embark
    and entrain,
Tally, transport, and deliver duly the Sons of Mary by land and
    main.

In an essay written many years ago, which remains one of the best studies of Kipling that we have, Colonel Bonamy Dobrée pointed out how constantly worldly success is disparaged; and that even the man who is an utter failure in life (and a gallery of such human wreckage can be assembled from among Kipling's characters) may be a nobler figure than the man who has successfully feathered his own nest. The moralist is always present, even in those tales of "The Jungle Book" which are taken by many readers to be merely fantasies to amuse the very young. It may be the moralist in Kipling that is displeasing to those intellectuals who have belittled him in my time. He was well aware that the moral is unwelcome, and must be insinuated, or conveyed (as we say nowadays) subliminally. This is explicit in "The Fabulists":

When all the world would keep a matter hid,
   Since Truth is seldom friend to any crowd,
Men write in fable as old Aesop did,
   Jesting at that which none will name aloud.
And this they needs must do, or it will fall
   Unless they please they are not heard at all.

It is only by keeping in mind Kipling the moralist and Kipling the seer that we can, I think, consider his politics. With his opinions, except as found in his published works, I am not concerned—only with his poems and his stories. Kipling was not a party man. Nor had he—and this is important—a mind gifted for abstract thought: he thought in images. He was not a philosopher, and his political philosophy is all in his firm and simple code of behaviour. What he has to say about politics may be summed up in "The Gods of the Copy-Book Headings":

In the Carboniferous Epoch we were promised abundance for all,
By robbing selected Peter to pay for collective Paul;
But, though we had plenty of money, there was nothing our money
   could buy,
And the Gods of the Copy-Book Headings said: *if you don't work
   you die.*

But Kipling was something rarer than a philosopher, he was a prophet. (Remember how long ago he wrote "The Man Who Was," and "The Truce of the Bear.") His mind was intuitive, rather than ratiocinative. His genius, if I understand it at all, lay in his powers of observation, description and intuition. That there is something a little *uncanny* in it all, even in his power of observation, is illustrated by an anecdote which I was told in Cambridge, and which may not be widely known. When he paid his first visit to Magdalene College, on being made an Honorary Fellow, he expressed a wish to view the Pepys Library and the manuscript of Pepys' dairy. The College, knowing that Kipling was a man who asked questions, and whose questions were apt to be unexpected and unanswerable, had assembled all the available scholars learned about Pepys and his time. Kipling asked the one question for which they were unprepared: what was the formula for the ink that Pepys used? He observed that it was dissimilar to that of any manuscript of the period that he had seen. The matter was looked into later, and it was found that Pepys had used an ink made by a formula of his own invention. And we all know the story of the Roman Legion which he placed at Hadrian's Wall.

I suggest that the fact that Kipling was an intuitive and not an intellectual, may go to account for his being underrated by intellectuals who are not intuitives. He had a gift of prophecy, and he must have appreciated the frustration of Cassandra. He foresaw two wars. That of 1914 is foreshadowed in his Ode to France written in 1913. And in 1932 he foresaw, in "The Storm Cone," the storm that was to burst seven years later, three years after his death. In his last years he regarded the future of the world with more and more misgiving. He seems to me the greatest English man of letters of his generation. Before lifting my glass I should like to quote in full, as a reminder of the man, the short poem which concludes his volume of verse—a poem of which I should like to have been the author:

> If I have given you delight
>   By aught that I have done,
> Let me lie quiet in that night
>   Which shall be yours anon:
>
> And for the little, little span
>   The dead are borne in mind,
> Seek not to question other than
>   The books I leave behind.

Ladies and gentlemen, I give you The Unfading Genius of Rudyard Kipling.

J. M. S. Tompkins

[The Structure of Revenge in
"Dayspring Mishandled"] *

IT CAN BE SAID of Kipling's revenge-tales, as it is said of Swinburne's love-poems, that the object of the emotion is not really there; that is, he is there as an inflammatory presence, a detested source of effects, but not as a person. Since the action of hatred is to sharpen the vision as to details but to obliterate the total personality of its object, this is no ground of complaint against a writer of short stories, but it is true that there is no genuine interrelation of hater and hated in any of the tales I have mentioned. They are never in prolonged proximity to each other, except in 'The Wrong Thing,' where the obsession is all on one side and is to be resolved in the end. Once only, in the superb 'Dayspring Mishandled,' did he undertake this aspect of his theme, and here only he makes his avenger a man of letters. The tale may perhaps be read, with due reserve, as a comment on the imagination that had conceived all the other tales of revenge, but this must be done 'in Feare and Decencie,' as Kipling said his father had taught him to portray "that Rare and Terrible Mystery . . . Man," when he dedicated In Black and White to him.

The tale is very tightly written. There are no flourishes in it; every sentence tells and matters. The writing is of that "infolded" sort which, at first reading, may seem to present a crumpled mass, but which gradually fills and spreads and tight-

* [From "Hatred and Revenge," *The Art of Rudyard Kipling* (London, 1959. Reprinted by permission of the author.]

ens with the fullness and tension of its meanings, until it is a
House of Life itself, a tent covering the erring and suffering
spirit of man. The title offers us two handles. It is a phrase
from the Chaucerian fragment that Manallace forges, as an
instrument of his revenge on Castorley, the Chaucer specialist;
it is also the condition of Manallace which has nourished that
revenge. He is the oak-spray of "Gertrude's Prayer," bruised
and knotted and twisted on itself in youth through his unhappy
love, which brings him nothing but the opportunity of nursing
and supporting a deserted and paralysed woman, whose eyes
look always for the husband who has left her. Thus his "dawn-
ing goth amiss," and when she dies, after many years, his life is
emptied, until it is filled by his secret hate for Castorley.

The structure of the tale does not declare itself till half-way
through. We seem to wander in various directions. The beginning looks back with desiderium to "the days beyond compare
and before the Judgments," and recreates Grayson and the
young men of his Fictional Supply Syndicate at supper at Neminaka's, where Manallace—"a darkish, slow northerner of the
type that does not ignite, but must be detonated"—fails to
come up to scratch with his consignment because it has "turned
into poetry on his hands," and Castorley, who "had gifts of
waking dislike," announces that he has inherited money and is
withdrawing from "hackwork" to follow "literature." A glance
at the older Manallace, bogged down in remunerative Wardour
Street romances "that exactly met, but never exceeded, every
expectation," covers the years to the War and the death of the
unnamed woman. A satiric sketch of Castorley, who has nursed
himself into the position of an international Chaucer expert—
Kipling is quite clear that the scholarship is genuine; it can even
at times break through his obsession with himself and "prove
how a man's work will try to save the soul of him"—brings us
to the point when he and Manallace meet again as temporary
Civil Servants, and to the short and unexplained scene when,
waiting together for a big air-raid, "the two men talked hu-
manly," and Manallace mentions the woman. Castorley, too,
had loved her "for a time . . . in his own way," and his proposal had been refused. Now "he said something in reply, and
from that hour—as was learned several years later—Manallace's

real life-work and interests began." But the tale turns away from this cryptic sign-post and seems to lose itself in detail about fifteenth century scribes and Manallace's "forlorn fancy" for trifles like a mediaeval recipe for ink, a Shetland quern and a battered Vulgate with rubricated initials. Then comes Castorley's great opportunity in the discovery of an unknown Chaucer fragment; and during the run of his excited volubility all that has preceded falls into place. Point by point, as he describes the contents of the fragment and the tests he has applied to it, Manallace's patient, deadly, year-long plotting comes to light; the "trifles" are seen as the necessary elements of his design, and the poem to derive from the Neminaka days of unspoilt hope. It is as if we had walked in a circle through high and pleasant brushwood, and, coming suddenly to an opening in it, find that we have all the time been circling the black and bitter pool of Manallace's hidden hate.

Castorley himself has provided the material with which the trap has been baited, for Manallace, who never denies his scholarship though he lures it on to treacherous ground, has sat at his feet for years, quietly provoking the display of the information he needs. The plan is to raise the expert to the height of celebrity and honour, and then—Manallace is not sure if it shall be public exposure, which may send him "off his veray parfit gentil nut" and shorten the revenge, or private blackmail, compelling him to uphold the forgery as long as he lives. At this point the unobtrusive "I," whose chief value has hitherto been to support Manallace morally by confirming the odiousness of his victim, asks: "What about your own position?" Manallace answers: "Oh—my position? I've been dead since—April, Fourteen,[1] it was." He thinks that his real life ended when the

---

[1] It was April, Fifteen, 'April of the first year of the War.' Kipling is never safe with dates. He complicates the dating of this tale by calling the woman Manallace loved 'Vidal's mother'. I can only suppose that he did this because names with him convey personality strongly, and she was to remain an impersonal object of devotion, particularized only through her sufferings. Vidal Benzaguen is a music-hall star in 'The Village that Voted the Earth was Flat' (published 1913). The *terminus a quo* is April 1891 when Dowson's 'Non sum qualis eram,' which Manallace quotes, came out. Manallace was then 'the boy' of the Neminaka group—say, twenty-two— and Vidal's mother was unmarried, since Castorley proposed to her. This makes Vidal a star at twenty and Manallace about forty-nine at the end of

woman he loved died. But the true answer comes some pages
later in the two verbs "groaned" and "shuddered," of which
Manallace is the subject. He is not dead, as he thought. His
soul is alive, and the "evil thing" begins to turn back on it. The
plot is ripe and his desire within his grasp, when two shadows
appear, which thicken rapidly into obstructions he cannot pass.
Castorley's wife, it seems, is indicating, as if it were "a sort of
joke" between them, that she sees through Manallace's plot
and would like to see it accomplished; and Castorley falls ill.
That a man should hesitate to strike a foe who is already
marked for death needs no explanation. The motive of Lady
Castorley's hints appears gradually. She is the mistress of
Gleeag, the surgeon who has operated on Castorley, and she is
impatient for her husband's death. It is she, not Manallace,
who has the really murderous mind, which is the reason that
the last sentence of the tale is given over to her satisfaction.
Worry is bad for Castorley, and she sees to it that he is worried,
urging the sick man on against time with the book on which
he and Manallace, now his "most valued assistant," are collab-
orating. Manallace has explicitly intended to kill his enemy, by
disgrace and the ruin of his ambition; but to revenge is one
thing and to be the tool of a disloyal woman's callous impa-
tience is quite another. Moreover, though this is never explicitly
stated, there is, in effect though not in intention, the bond of
shared work to hold him back. He postpones and evades. He
goes abroad; he mislays some essential material; he lures Castorley up by-paths of interest. He is now driven into the position
of protecting him; but there is no way out of the trap in which
he has caught himself.

> Manallace shuddered. 'If I stay abroad, I'm helping to kill him.
> If I help him to hurry up the book, I'm expected to kill him. *She*
> knows. . . . I'm not going to have him killed, though.'

---

the War. We must allow some years after that for the development of his
plot and his holidays in the Shetlands and Faroes and the Low Countries.
This fits Manallace very well, but makes Vidal a very youthful success in
her arduous profession. I doubt, however, if Kipling worked all this out, any
more than he worked out the connection between 'Mowgli's Brothers' and
'In the Rukh.' He thought of his own London years (1890–91) and then
of a noncommittal sobriquet for the woman.

He draws out their discussions; and Castorley grows worse. The atmosphere of the sick-room closes round us, and begins to vibrate with the apprehensions of the sick. It is clear that Castorley is being kept under drugs, and that his trouble is incurable. The last scene comes suddenly "in steam perfumed with Friar's Balsam." Castorley's confused mind, rambling through all the layers of past and present, throws up with acute distress the misgivings his wife has implanted in him, his complete distrust of her, and, from very deep down, the hidden, denied sense of guilt and remorse about the woman who rejected him.

There was an urgent matter to be set right, and now that he had The Title and knew his own mind it would all end happily and he would be well again. Please would we let him go out, just to speak to—he named her; he named her by her 'little' name out of the old Neminaka days.

Again and again he appeals to Manallace, and Manallace, shaken, answers the appeals with reassurances. Then "his pain broke through all the drugs, and the outcry filled the room." Gleeag, telephoning the news of his patient's death to the narrator next morning, says: "Perhaps it's just as well. . . . We might have come across something we couldn't have coped with. . . . We let him through as easily as possible." This is exactly what Manallace has done, in both respects. Our last sight of him is at the Crematorium, taking out his black gloves. He has bound on his own shoulders the burden meant for Castorley's, by insisting to Lady Castorley that the book must be published. "She is going to be known as his widow—for a while, at any rate," he says with spleen against the human hand that has helped to disarm him.

The question arises—and was meant to arise, I think— whether Manallace, even if his course had remained uncomplicated, could ever have "pull[ed] the string of the shower-bath." He is not one of Kipling's prompt young men. During the War he was of age to be assigned to the Office of Co-ordinated Supervisals, and by the end of the tale he is in his fifties. His reaction to his first suspicions of Castorley's wife is not to get his blow in first, but to evolve refinements of his plan. "He wrapped himself lovingly and leisurely round his new task." Moreover he is a man of letters. It is naturally in the realm of the imagination that he constructs, and he can find satisfaction there. All the more is he subject to the reprisals of the spirit he has raised, a spirit ironic and deadly. He has not accomplished his revenge, except in thought, or forgiven Castorley. It has been his "interest." He has let the Poison-tree root in his heart, and has nourished it with his grief and his deceit. But the enemy is not dead beneath the tree, as in Blake's poem; he is struck down by another agency, outside the circle of the branches. The upas crumbles, and Manallace is left "emptied out" by hate, as he had been by his sacrificial love. It is a Limit, but there is no sign of another Renewal.

This view finds support if we follow Nodier's song of the mandragora, at the head of the tale, to its source in his fairy-story "La Fée aux Miettes." [2] In his preface to this story, Nodier tells us that he thinks the only way in which a fantastic tale can gain sufficient credence to be enjoyed in a sceptical age is to cause it to be told by a lunatic to a melancholic. This surprising recipe results in an introductory passage in which the melancholic, visiting the botanic gardens attached to a madhouse, finds a bed of mandragoras, largely uprooted and withered. He recalls that the mandragora is a powerful narcotic, "propre à endormir les douleurs des misérables qui végètent sous ces murailles," and, plucking one, he addresses it as a power that carries into suffering souls a forgetfulness sweeter than sleep and almost as impassible as death. At this a young man rises from the ground, begging to know if the mandragora has spoken, if it has sung the song of the mandragora, whose single verse he repeats:

> C'est moi, c'est moi, c'est moi!
> Je suis la Mandragore!
> La fille des beaux jours qui s'éveille a l'aurore—
> Et qui chante pour toi!

When he is told that it is voiceless, like all other mandragoras, he takes it and drops it on the ground, saying: "Then this is not yet the one." We need not consider the tale he tells, for to Nodier the mandragora symbolizes poetical delusion, not hatred, and this has no bearing on Kipling's work. At the end,

---

2 I owe this reference to my colleague, Miss G. E. Brereton.

however, the melancholic, leaving the madhouse, meets a doctor who discourses with repellent pedantry on the nature of the plant. It is somniferous and poisonous. Its narcotic, anodyne, refrigerative and hypnotic properties have been known since the time of Hippocrates. It can be used with success in cases of melancholy, and the juice of its root and rind is a powerful emeto-cathartic, which, however, more often occasions death than a cure.

This symbolism, appropriate to poetical delusion, becomes immensely more powerful when it is applied to revenge. This is the narcotic that Manallace finds for his empty and aching life. Since its origin is in the "dayspring" and good days of his youth, it is indeed "la fille des beaux jours." It is anodyne, refrigerative, hypnotic. It cradles him in delusions for a while. But it is not the right mandragora and he lets it fall. Even the words of the doctor fit this meaning. Revengeful hatred is a powerful cathartic that can empty the mind of other pains, but it is more often deadly than sanative to the mind that entertains it.

We have, then a double reversal in our attitude to Manallace's quietly absorbed activity. His disconnected occupations, before we understand their object, are "forlorn fancies." When we understand it, they are suddenly seen to be purposive and part of a formidable intention. In the last stage, the whole scheme becomes again a "forlorn fancy," a self-delusion, a narcotic that has lost its power. Nothing of the black dream is realized. One may say that it has had no effect on Castorley's life or death, except the ironically inverted effects of procuring him the recognition he thirsted for, putting Manallace into close relations with him and turning him into Castorley's defender. By this means he becomes aware at last of the strangled guilt and regret at the bottom of Castorley's mind, which, if he had known it earlier, would have prevented him from conceiving his purpose. Not even devils, but only delusions, have filled the empty house. It is Manallace alone who is poisoned by the mandragora; and it is not the right one.

The force of this conception is much increased by the nature of the man who yields to this deadly indulgence. The tale is written with such drastic and sober economy that the reader is sometimes put to it to trace a strong impression to its source;

but the suggestion of charm that hangs about Manallace seems
to derive from one or two pleasant turns of phrase, such as "a
day's gadzooking and vital-stapping," and from the conviction
we receive of the narrator's unexpressed affection for him. All
the emotions are kept battened down through the tale, except
Castorley's which are liberally displayed. His skinless irritability,
his overt malice and mean revenges, his craving appetite for
importance are fully lighted. Manallace's long, agonizing service
to the woman he loves is indicated only by her living eyes in
her paralysed body, looking away from him, and by his renunciation of his literary ambitions; and this last is manifest only if
we compare his cheerfully gruff refusal to "write a real book"—
"I've got my label and I'm not going to chew it off"—with the
Neminaka days, long ago, when he was possessed, and "was"
Chaucer for a week. He gives away very little, while we watch
him, and for pages he is removed from us. It follows, then, that
an occasional adverb—"weakly," "unsteadily,"—attached to
something he says, has a condensed, informative power beyond
the usual force of the word, and that "groaned" and "shuddered"
reverberate like thunder in an abyss. I cannot explain the effect
of the black gloves at the end; it is like the occulting of a personality. Kipling, on the last page of a highly intellectualized
tale, regains for a moment his spontaneous imaginative stroke.

Nothing hangs loose or is dropped. The "something unpleas-
ant" that Castorley wanted to say at Neminaka's, but was sup-
pressed, breaks out during his delirium in a "full, high, affected
voice, unheard for a generation." The negress in yellow satin
outside the old Empire, who seems, when she is mentioned, a
mere decorative blob of colour, is locked into the pattern when
we learn, much later, that what the young and tipsy Manallace
had said to her was that he had been faithful, Cynara, in his
fashion. The grave and responsible irony in which the tale is
drenched fills the key-sentences brimful. One of these comes in
a couplet of Manallace's forgery:

> Let all men change as Fortune may send,
> But Knighthood beareth service to the end.

Castorley praises this as a "splendid appeal for the spirit of
chivalry," approving in literature what he denies in life; and by

this time Manallace's service to the dead woman has taken strange shapes. A sort of refrain is introduced when Manallace says casually about his "jocundly-sentimental" romances: "If you save people thinking, you can do anything with them." It is redirected as a comment on Castorley's rising reputation, and finally, weighted now with its full meaning, launched by Lady Castorley to its quivering target in her husband's self-esteem. This detail becomes tedious; but the tale has been much undervalued and misunderstood. It has even been called a structural tangle. It seems to me one of Kipling's great achievements. To analyse its patterns, as I have done, may give a false suggestion of rigidity and echoing emphasis. This is far from the case; all the exactly articulated detail is carried on a flowing and natural movement, and largely by the entirely convincing voices of the two men. There is in this tale, as Voiron says of Apis's performance in the bull-ring at Arles, "a breadth of technique that comes of reasoned art, and, above all, the passion that arrives after experience." The passion, however, and the compassion are implied, not expressed. It is, I suppose, an elderly tale, with its long retrospects and its quiet acceptance of human error and wastage, but it is certainly not cold, and very far from enfeebled. When it has once been fairly read, it is unforgettable. All its details are instinct with life, and, like seeds, throw up fresh growth as the years pass. The process does not stop with the solution of the "enigma," any more than our sense of the strangeness of a particular fate stops when we know what happened to a man and what he did.

Randall Jarrell

On Preparing to Read Kipling*

MARK TWAIN said that it isn't what they don't know that hurts people, it's what they do know that isn't so. This is true of Kipling. If people don't know about Kipling they can read Kipling, and then they'll know about Kipling: it's ideal. But most people already do know about Kipling—not very much, but too much: they know what isn't so, or what might just as well not be so, it matters so little. They know that, just as Calvin Coolidge's preacher was against sin and the Snake was for it, Kipling was for imperialism; he talked about the white man's burden; he was a crude popular—immensely popular—writer who got popular by writing "If," and "On the Road to Mandalay," and "The Jungle Book," and stories about India like Somerset Maugham, and children's stories; he wrote, "East is East and West is West and never the twain shall meet"; he wrote, "The female of the species is more deadly than the male"—or was that Pope? *Somebody* wrote it. In short: Kipling was someone people used to think was wonderful, but we know better than that now.

People certainly didn't know better than that then. "Dear Harry," William James begins. (It is hard to remember, hard to believe, that anyone ever called Henry James *Harry*, but if it had to be done, William James was the right man to do it.)

* [From *A Sad Heart At the Supermarket* (New York, 1962), pp. 114–139. First printed as the Introduction to *The Best Short Stories of Rudyard Kipling* (New York, 1961). Reprinted by permission of Doubleday & Co., Inc.]

"Last Sunday I dined with Howells at the Childs', and was delighted to hear him say that you were both a friend and an admirer of Rudyard Kipling. I am ashamed to say that I have been ashamed to write of that infant phenomenon, not knowing, with your exquisitely refined taste, how you might be affected by him and fearing to *jar*. [It is wonderful *to have the engineer/Hoist with his own petard*.] The more rejoiced am I at this, but why didn't you say so ere now? He's more of a Shakespeare than anyone yet in this generation of ours, as it strikes me. And seeing the new effects he lately brings in in "The Light that Failed," and that Simla Ball story with Mrs. Hauksbee in the *Illustrated London News*, makes one sure now that he is only at the beginning of a rapidly enlarging career, with indefinite growth before him. Much of his present coarseness and jerkiness is youth only, divine youth. But *what* a youth! Distinctly the biggest literary phenomenon of our time. He has such human entrails, and he takes less time to get under the heartstrings of his personages than anyone I know. On the whole, bless him.

"All intellectual work is the same,—the artist feeds the public on his own bleeding insides. Kant's *Kritik* is just like a Strauss waltz, and I felt the other day, finishing "The Light that Failed," and an ethical address to be given at Yale College simultaneously, that there was no *essential* difference between Rudyard Kipling and myself as far as that sacrificial element goes."

It surprises us to have James take Kipling so seriously, without reservations, with Shakespeare—to treat him as if he were Kant's *Kritik* and not a Strauss waltz. (Even Henry James, who could refer to "the good little Thomas Hardy"—who was capable of applying to the Trinity itself the adjective *poor*—somehow felt that he needed for Kipling that coarse word *genius*, and called him, at worst "the great little Kipling.") Similarly, when Goethe and Matthew Arnold write about Byron, we are surprised to see them bringing in Shakespeare—are surprised to see how unquestioningly, with what serious respect, they speak of Byron, as if he were an ocean or a new ice age: "our soul," wrote Arnold, "had *felt* him like the thunder's roll." It is as though mere common sense, common humanity, required this of them: the existence of a world-figure like Byron demands (as the existence of a good or great writer does not) that any inhabitant of the world treat him somehow as the world treats him. Goethe knew that Byron "is a child when he reflects," but this did not prevent him from treating Byron exactly as he treated that other world-figure Napoleon.

An intelligent man said that the world felt Napoleon as a weight, and that when he died it would give a great *oof* of relief. This is just as true of Byron, or of such Byrons of their days as Kipling and Hemingway: after a generation or two the world is tired of being their pedestal, shakes them off with an *oof*, and then—hoisting onto its back a new world-figure—feels the penetrating satisfaction of having made a mistake all its own. Then for a generation or two the Byron lies in the dust where we left him: if the old world did him more than justice, a new one does him less. "If he was so good as all that why isn't he still famous?" the new world asks—if it asks anything. And then when another generation or two are done, we decide that he wasn't altogether a mistake people made in those days, but a real writer after all—that if we like *Childe Harold* a good deal less than anyone thought of liking it then, we like *Don Juan* a good deal more. Byron *was* a writer, people just didn't realize the sort of writer he was. We can feel impatient with Byron's world for liking him for the wrong reasons, and with the succeeding world for disliking him for the wrong reasons, and we are glad that our world, the real world, has at last settled Byron's account.

Kipling's account is still unsettled. Underneath, we still hold it against him that the world quoted him in its sleep, put him in its headlines when he was ill, acted as if he were God; we are glad that we have Hemingway instead, to put in *our* headlines when his plane crashes. Kipling is in the dust, and the dust seems to us a very good place for him. But in twenty or thirty years, when Hemingway is there instead, and we have a new Byron-Kipling-Hemingway to put in our news-programs when his rocket crashes, our resistance to Hemingway will have taken the place of our resistance to Kipling, and we shall find

ourselves willing to entertain the possibility that Kipling *was* a
writer after all—people just didn't realize the sort of writer he
was.

There is a way of travelling into this future—of realizing, now,
the sort of writer Kipling was—that is unusually simple, but that
people are unusually unwilling to take. The way is: to read
Kipling as if one were not prepared to read Kipling; as if one
didn't already know about Kipling—had never been told how
readers do feel about Kipling, should feel about Kipling; as if
one were setting out, naked, to see something that is there
naked. I don't entirely blame the reader if he answers: "Thanks
very much; if it's just the same to you, I'll keep my clothes on."
It's only human of him—man is the animal that wears clothes.
Yet aren't works of art in some sense a way of doing without
clothes, a means by which reader, writer, and subject are able
for once to accept their own nakedness? the nakedness not
merely of the "naked truth," but also of the naked wishes that
come before and after that truth? To read Kipling, for once,
not as the crudely effective, popular writer we know him to
be, but as, perhaps, the something else that even crudely effective, popular writers can become, would be to exhibit a magna-
nimity that might do justice both to Kipling's potentialities and
to our own. Kipling did have, at first, the "coarseness and jerkiness" and mannered vanity of youth, human youth; Kipling
did begin as a reporter, did print in newspapers the *Plain Tales
from the Hills* which ordinary readers—and, unfortunately, most
extraordinary ones—do think typical of his work; but then for
half a century he kept writing. Chekhov began by writing jokes
for magazines, skits for vaudeville; Shakespeare began by writing
Titus Andronicus and *The Two Gentlemen of Verona*, some of
the crudest plays any crudely effective, popular writer has ever
turned out. Kipling is neither a Chekhov nor a Shakespeare, but
he is far closer to both than to the clothing-store-dummy-with-
the-solar-topee we have agreed to call Kipling. Kipling, like it or
not, admit it or not, was a great genius; and a great neurotic;
and a great professional, one of the most skillful writers who
have ever existed—one of the writers who have used English
best, one of the writers who most often have made other writers
exclaim, in the queer tone they used for the exclamation:

"Well, I've got to admit it really is *written*." When he died and was buried in that foreign land England, that only the Anglo-Indians know, I wish that they had put above his grave, there in *their* Westminster Abbey: "It really was *written*."

Mies van der Rohe said, very beautifully: "I don't want to be interesting, I want to be good." Kipling, a great realist but a greater inventor, could have said that he didn't want to be realistic, he wanted to get it right: that he wanted it not the way it did or—statistics show—does happen, but the way it really would happen. You often feel about something in Shakespeare or Dostoievsky that nobody ever said such a thing, but that it's just the sort of thing people would say if they could— is more real, in some sense, than what people do say. If you have given your imagination free rein, let things go as far as they want to go, the world they made for themselves while you watched can have, for you and later watchers, a spontaneous finality. Some of Kipling has this spontaneous finality; and because he has written so many different kinds of stories—no writer of fiction of comparable genius has depended so much, for so long, on short stories alone—you end dazzled by his variety of realization: so many plants, and so many of them dewy!

If I had to pick one writer to invent a conversation between an animal, a god, and a machine, it would be Kipling. To discover what, if they ever said, the dumb would say—this takes real imagination; and this imagination of what isn't is the extension of a real knowledge of what is, the knowledge of a consummate observer who took no notes, except of names and dates: "if a thing didn't stay in my memory I argued it was hardly worth writing out." Knowing what the peoples, animals, plants, weathers of the world look like, sound like, smell like, was Kipling's *métier*, and so was knowing the words that could make someone else know. You can argue about the judgment he makes of something, but the thing is there. When as a child you first begin to read, what attracts you to a book is illustrations and conversations, and what scares you away is "long descriptions." In Kipling illustration and conversation and description (not long description; read, even the longest of his descriptions is short) have merged into a "toothsome amalgam" which the child reads with a grown-up's ease, and the grown-up with a child's wonder. Often Kipling writes with such grace and command, such a combination of experienced mastery and congenital inspiration, that we repeat with Goethe: "Seeing someone accomplishing arduous things with ease gives us an impression of witnessing the impossible." Sometimes the arduous thing Kipling is accomplishing seems to us a queer, even an absurd thing for anyone to wish to accomplish. But don't we have to learn to consent to this, with Kipling as with other good writers?—to consent to the fact that good writers just don't have good sense; that they are going to write it their way, not ours; that they are never going to have the objective, impersonal rightness they should have, but only the subjective, personal wrongness from which we derived the idea of the rightness. The first thing we notice about *War and Peace* and *Madame Bovary* and *Remembrance of Things Past* is how wonderful they are; the second thing we notice is how much they have wrong with them. They are not at all the perfect work of art we want—so perhaps Ruskin was right when he said that the person who wants perfection knows nothing about art.

Kipling says about a lion cub he and his family had on the Cape: "He dozed on the stoep, I noticed, due north and south, looking with slow eyes up the length of Africa"; this, like several thousand such sentences, makes you take for granted the truth of his "I made my own experiments in the weights, colors, perfumes, and attributes of words in relation to other words, either as read aloud so that they may hold the ear, or, scattered over the page, draw the eye." His words range from gaudy effectiveness to perfection; he is a professional magician but, also, a magician. He says about stories: "A tale from which pieces have been raked out is like a fire that has been poked. One does not know that the operation has been performed, but everyone feels the effect." (He even tells you how best to rake out the pieces: with a brush and Chinese ink you grind yourself.) He is a kind of Liszt—so isn't it just empty bravura, then? Is Liszt's? Sometimes; but sometimes bravura is surprisingly full, sometimes virtuosos are surprisingly plain: to boil a potato perfectly takes a chef home from the restaurant for the day.

Kipling was just such a potato-boiler: a professional knower of professionals, a great trapeze-artist, cabinet-maker, prestidigitator, with all the unnumbered details of others' guilds, crafts, mysteries, techniques at the tip of his fingers—or, at least, at the tip of his tongue. The first sentences he could remember saying as a child had been haltingly translated into English "from the vernacular" (that magical essential phrase for the reader of Kipling!) and just as children feel that it is they and not the grown-ups who see the truth, so Kipling felt about many things that it is the speakers of the vernacular and not the sahibs who tell the truth; that there are many truths that, to be told at all, take the vernacular. From childhood on he learned—to excess or obsession, even—the vernaculars of earth, the worlds inside the world, the many species into which place and language and work divide man. From the species which the division of labor produces it is only a step to the animal species which evolutionary specialization produces, so that Kipling finds it easy to write stories about animals; from the vernaculars or dialects or cants which place or profession produces (Kipling's slogan is, almost, "The cant *is* the man") it is only a step to those which time itself produces, so that Kipling finds it easy to write stories about all the different provinces of the past, or the future (in "As Easy as ABC"), or Eternity (if his queer institutional stories of the bureaucracies of Heaven and Hell are located there). Kipling was no Citizen of the World, but like the Wandering Jew he had lived in many places and known many peoples, an uncomfortable stranger repeating to himself the comforts of earth, all its immemorial contradictory ways of being at home.

Goethe, very winningly, wanted to have put on his grave a sentence saying that he had never been a member of any guild, and was an amateur until the day he died. Kipling could have said, "I never saw the guild I wasn't a member of," and was a professional from the day he first said to his *ayah*, in the vernacular—not being a professional myself, I don't know what it was he said, but it was the sort of thing a man would say who, from the day he was sixteen till the day he was twenty-three, was always—"luxury of which I dream still!"—shaved by his servant before he woke up in the morning.

This fact of his life, I've noticed, always makes hearers give a little shiver; but it is all the mornings when no one shaved Kipling before Kipling woke up, because Kipling had never been to sleep, that make me shiver. "Such night-wakings" were "laid upon me through my life," Kipling writes, and tells you in magical advertising prose how lucky the wind before dawn always was for him. You and I should have such luck! Kipling was a professional, but a professional possessed by both the Dæmon he tells you about, who writes some of the stories for him, and the demons he doesn't tell you about, who write some others. Nowadays we've learned to call part of the unconscious *it* or *id*; Kipling had not, but he called this Personal Demon of his *it*. (When he told his father that *Kim* was finished his father asked: "Did *it* stop, or you?" Kipling "told him that it was It.") "When your Dæmon is in charge," Kipling writes, "do not try to think consciously. Drift, wait, and obey." He was sure of the books in which "my Dæmon was with me . . . When those books were finished they said so themselves with, almost, the water-hammer click of a tap turned off." (Yeats said that a poem finishes itself with a click like a closing box.) Kipling speaks of the "doom of the makers": when their Dæmon is missing they are no better than anybody else; but when he is there, and they put down what he dictates, "the work he gives shall continue, whether in earnest or jest." Kipling even "learned to distinguish between the peremptory motions of my Dæmon, and the 'carry-over' of induced electricity, which comes of what you might call mere 'frictional' writing." We always tend to distrust geniuses about genius, as if what they say didn't arouse much empathy in us, or as if we were waiting till some more reliable source of information came along; still, isn't what Kipling writes a colored version of part of the plain truth?—there is plenty of supporting evidence. But it is interesting to me to see how thoroughly Kipling manages to avoid any subjective guilt, fallible human responsibility, so that he can say about anything in his stories either: "Entirely conscious and correct, objectively established, independently corroborated, the experts have testified, the professionals agree, it is the consensus of the authorities at the Club," or else: "I had nothing to do with it. I know nothing about it. *It* did it. The Dæmon did it all." The reader of Kipling—this reader at least—hates to give all the

credit to the Professional or to the Dæmon; perhaps the demons had something to do with it too. Let us talk about the
demons.

One writer says that we only notice what hurts us—that if
you went through the world without hurting anyone, nobody
would even know you had been alive. This is quite false, but
true, too: if you put it in terms of the derivation of the Principle of Reality from the primary Principle of Pleasure, it does
not even sound shocking. But perhaps we only notice a sentence
if it sounds shocking—so let me say grotesquely: Kipling was
someone who had spent six years in a concentration camp as a
child; he never got over it. As a very young man he spent seven
years in an India that confirmed his belief in concentration
camps; he never got over this either.

As everybody remembers, one of Goya's worst engravings has
underneath it: *I saw it.* Some of Kipling has underneath: *It is
there.* Since the world is a necessary agreement that it isn't
there, the world answered: *It isn't,* and told Kipling what a
wonderful imagination he had. Part of the time Kipling answered stubbornly: *I've been there* (*I am there* would have
been even truer) and part of the time he showed the world what
a wonderful imagination he had. Say *Fairy-tales!* enough to a
writer and he will write you fairy-tales. But to our *Are you telling me the truth or are you reassuring yourself?*—we ask it often
of any writer, but particularly often of Kipling—he sometimes
can say truthfully: *Reassuring you;* we and Kipling have interests in common. Kipling knew that "every nation, like every
individual, walks in a vain show—else it could not live with
itself"; Kipling knew people's capacity not to see: "through all
this shifting, shouting brotheldom the pious British house-
holder and his family bored their way back from the theaters,
eyes-front and fixed, as though not seeing." But he himself had
seen, and so believed in, the City of Dreadful Night, and the
imperturbable or delirious or dying men who ran the city; this
City outside was the duplicate of the City inside; and when
the people of Victorian Europe didn't believe in any of it,
except as you believe in a ghost story, he knew that this was
only because they didn't *know*—he knew. So he was obsessed
by—wrote about, dreamed about, and stayed awake so as not

to dream about—many concentration camps, of the soul as well
as of the body; many tortures, hauntings, hallucinations, de-
liria, diseases, nightmares, practical jokes, revenges, monsters,
insanities, neuroses, abysses, forlorn hopes, last chances, extrem-
ities of every kind; these and their sweet opposites. He feels
the convalescent's gratitude for mere existence, that the world
is what the world was: how blue the day is, to the eye that has
been blinded! Kipling praises the cessation of pain and its more
blessed accession, when the body's anguish blots out for a little
"Life's grinning face . . . the trusty Worm that dieth not, the
steadfast Fire also." He praises man's old uses, home and all
the ways of home: its Father and Mother, there to run to if you
could only wake; and praises all our dreams of waking, our
fantasies of return or revenge or insensate endurance. He praises
the words he has memorized, that man has made from the
silence; the senses that cancel each other out, that man has
made from the senselessness; the worlds man has made from the
world; but he praises and reproduces the sheer charm of—few
writers are so purely charming!—the world that does not need
to have anything done to it, that is simply there around us as
we are there in it. He knows the joy of finding exactly the right
words for what there are no words for; the satisfactions of sentimentality and brutality and love too, the "exquisite tenderness" that began in cruelty. But in the end he thanks God
most for the small drugs that last—is grateful that He has not
laid on us "the yoke of too long Fear and Wonder," but has
given us Habit and Work: so that his Seraphs waiting at the
Gate praise God

> Not for any miracle of easy Loaves and Fishes
> But for doing, 'gainst our will, work against our
>   wishes,
> Such as finding food to fill daily emptied dishes . . .

praise him

> Not for Prophecies or Powers, Visions, Gifts, or
>   Graces
> But the unregardful hours that grind us in our places
> With the burden on our backs, the weather in our
>   faces.

"Give me the first six years of a child's life and you can have the rest" are the first words of *Something of Myself*, Kipling's reticent and revealing autobiography. The sentence exactly fits and exactly doesn't fit. For the first six years of his life the child lived in Paradise, the inordinately loved and reasonably spoiled son of the best of parents; after that he lived in the Hell in which the best of parents put him, and paid to have him kept: in "a dark land, and a darker room full of cold, in one wall of which a woman made naked fire . . . a woman who took in children whose parents were in India." The child did not see his parents again for the next six years. He accepted the Hell as "eternally established . . . I had never heard of Hell, so I was introduced to it in all its terrors . . . I was regularly beaten . . . I have known a certain amount of bullying, but this was calculated torture—religious as well as scientific . . . Deprivation from reading was added to my punishments . . . I was well beaten and sent to school through the streets of Southsea with the placard "Liar" between my shoulders . . . Some sort of nervous breakdown followed, for I imagined I saw shadows and things that were not there, and they worried me more than the Woman . . . A man came down to see me as to my eyes and reported that I was half-blind. This, too, was supposed to be 'showing-off,' and I was segregated from my sister—another punishment—as a sort of moral leper."

At the end of the six years the best of parents came back for their leper ("she told me afterwards that when she first came up to my room to kiss me goodnight, I flung up an arm to guard off the cuff I had been trained to expect"), and for the rest of their lives they continued to be the best and most loving of parents, blamed by Kipling for nothing, adored by Kipling for everything: "I think I can truthfully say that those two made up for me the only public for whom then I had any regard whatever till their deaths, in my forty-fifth year."

My *best of parents* cannot help sounding ironic, yet I do not mean it as irony. From the father's bas-reliefs for *Kim* to the mother's "There's no Mother in Poetry, my dear," when the son got angry at her criticism of his poems—from beginning to end they are bewitching; you cannot read about them with-

out wanting to live with them; they were the best of parents.
It is *this* that made Kipling what he was: if they had been the
worst of parents, even fairly bad parents, even ordinary parents,
it would all have made sense, Kipling himself could have made
sense out of it. As it was, his world had been torn in two and
he himself torn in two: for under the part of him that extenuated everything, blamed for nothing, there was certainly
a part that extenuated nothing, blamed for everything—a part
whose existence he never admitted, most especially not to himself. He says about some of the things that happened to him
during those six years: "In the long run these things and many
more of the like drained me of any capacity for real, personal
hatred for the rest of my life." To admit from the unconscious
something inadmissible, one can simply deny it, bring it up
into the light with a *No*; Kipling has done so here—the capacity for real, personal hatred, real, personal revenge, summary
fictional justice, is plain throughout Kipling's work. Listen to
him tell how he first began to write. He has just been told
about Dante: "I bought a fat, American-cloth-bound notebook
and set to work on an *Inferno*, into which I put, under appropriate tortures, all my friends and most of the masters."
(Why only *most?* Two were spared, one for the Father and
one for the Mother.) Succinct and reticent as *Something of
Myself* is, it has room for half a dozen scenes in which the
helpless Kipling is remorselessly, systematically, comprehensively
humiliated before the inhabitants of his universe. At school,
for instance: "H—— then told me off before my delighted
companions in his best style, which was acid and contumelious.
He wound up with a few general remarks about dying as a
'scurrilous journalist' . . . The tone, matter, and setting of
his discourse were as brutal as they were meant to be—brutal
as the necessary wrench on the curb that fetches up a too-
flippant colt." Oh, necessary, entirely necessary, we do but
torture in education! one murmurs to these methodical justifi-
cations of brutality as methodical, one of authority's necessary
stages. Here is another master: "Under him I came to feel
that words could be used as weapons, for he did me the honor
to talk at me plentifully . . . One learns more from a good
scholar in a rage than from a score of lucid and laborious

drudges; and to be made the butt of one's companions in full
form is no bad preparation for later experiences. I think this
'approach' is now discouraged for fear of hurting the soul of
youth, but in essence it is no more than rattling tins or firing
squibs under a colt's nose. I remember nothing save satisfaction
or envy when C—— broke his precious ointments over my
head." Nothing? Better for Kipling if he had remembered—
not remembering gets rid of nothing. Yet who knows? he may
even have felt—known that he felt—"nothing save satisfaction
and envy," the envying satisfaction of identification. As he
says, he was learning from a master to use words as weapons,
but he had already learned from his life a more difficult lesson:
to know that, no matter how the sick heart and raw being
rebel, it is all for the best; in the past there were the best of
masters and in the future there will be the best of masters,
if only we can wait out, bear out, the brutal present—the incomprehensible present that some day we shall comprehend
as a lesson.

The scene changes from England to India, school to Club,
but the action—passion, rather—is the same: "As I entered
the long, shabby dining-room where we all sat at one table,
everybody hissed. I was innocent enough to ask: 'What's the
joke? Who are they hissing?' 'You,' said the man at my side.
'Your damn rag has ratted over the Bill.' It is not pleasant to
sit still when one is twenty while all your universe hisses you."
One expects next a sentence about how customary and salutary
hissing is for colts, but for once it doesn't come; and when
Kipling's syntax suffers as it does in this sentence, he is remembering something that truly is not pleasant. He even
manages somewhat to justify, somehow to justify, his six years
in Hell: the devils' inquisitions, after all, "made me give attention to the lies I soon found it necessary to tell; and this,
I presume, is the foundation of literary effort . . . Nor was my
life an unsuitable preparation for my future, in that it demanded constant wariness, the habit of observation and at-
tendance on moods and tempers; the noting of discrepancies
between speech and action; a certain reserve of demeanor; and
automatic suspicion of sudden favors." I have seen writers
called God's spies, but Kipling makes it sound as if they were

just spies—or spies on God. If only he could have blamed God—
his Gods—a little consciously, forgiven them a little unconsciously! could have felt that someone, sometimes, doesn't
mean something to happen! But inside, and inside stories, everything is meant.

After you have read Kipling's fifty or seventy-five best stories
you realize that few men have written this many stories of
this much merit, and that very few have written more and better
stories. Chekhov and Turgenev are two who immediately come
to mind; and when I think of their stories I cannot help thinking of what seems to me the greatest lack in Kipling's. I don't
know exactly what to call it: a lack of dispassionate moral
understanding, perhaps—of the ability both to understand
things and to understand that there is nothing to do about
them. (In a story, after all, there is always something you *can*
do, something that a part of you is always trying to make you
do.) Kipling is a passionate moralist, with a detailed and occasionally profound knowledge of part of things; but his moral
spectrum has shifted, so that he can see far down into the
infra-red, but is blind for some frequencies normal eyes are
sensitive to. His morality is the one-sided, desperately pro-
tective, sometimes vindictive morality of someone who has
been for some time the occupant of one of God's concentration camps, and has had to spend the rest of his life justifying
or explaining out of existence what he cannot forget. Kipling
tries so hard to celebrate and justify true authority, the work
and habit and wisdom of the world, because he feels so bitterly
the abyss of pain and insanity that they overlie, and can do—
even will do—nothing to prevent.

Kipling's morality is the morality of someone who has to
prove that God is not responsible for part of the world, and
that the Devil is. If Father and Mother were not to blame for
anything, yet what did happen to you could happen to you—
if God is good, and yet the concentration camps exist—then
there has to be *someone* to blame, and to punish too, some
real, personal source of the world's evil. (He finishes "At the
End of the Passage" by having someone quote: "There may
be Heaven, there must be Hell./ Meanwhile there is our life
here. Well?" In most of his stories he sees to it that our life

here is Heaven and Hell.) But in this world, often, there is
nothing to praise but no one to blame, and Kipling can bear
to admit this in only a few of his stories. He writes about one
source of things in his childhood: "And somehow or other I
came across a tale about a lion-hunter in South Africa who fell
among lions who were all Freemasons, and with them entered
into a conspiracy against some wicked baboons. I think that,
too, lay dormant until the Jungle Books began to be born." In
Chekhov or Turgenev, somehow or other, the lions aren't really
Freemasons and the baboons aren't really wicked. In Chekhov
and Turgenev, in fact, most of the story has disappeared from
the story: there was a lion-hunter in South Africa, and first he
shot the lions, and then he shot the baboons, and finally he
shot himself; and yet it wasn't *wicked*, exactly, but human—
very human.

Kipling had learned too well and too soon that, in William
James' words: "The normal process of life contains moments
as bad as any of those which insane melancholy is filled with,
moments in which radical evil gets its innings and takes its
solid turn. The lunatic's visions of horror are all drawn from the
material of daily fact. Our civilization is founded on the sham-
bles, and each individual existence goes out in a lonely spasm
of helpless agony. If you protest, my friend, wait till you arrive there yourself!" Kipling had arrived there early and returned
there often. One thinks sadly of how deeply congenial to this
torturing obsessive knowledge of Kipling's the first World War
was: the death and anguish of Europe produced some of his
best and most terrible stories, and the death of his own son,
his own anguish, produced "Mary Postgate," that nightmare-ish,
most human and most real day-dream of personal revenge. The
world *was* Hell and India underneath, after all; and he could
say to the Victorian, Edwardian Europeans who had thought it
all just part of his style: "You wouldn't believe me!"

Svidrigaylov says: "We are always thinking of eternity as an
idea that cannot be understood, something immense. But why
must it be? What if, instead of all this, you suddenly find just
a little room there, something like a village bath-house, grimy,
and spiders in every corner, and that's all eternity is . . . I,
you know, would certainly have made it so deliberately." Part of

Kipling would have replied to this with something denunciatory and biblical, but another part would have blurted eagerly, like somebody out of *Kim:* "Oah yess, that is dam-well likely! Like a dâk-bungalow, you know." It is an idea that would have occurred to him, down to the last *deliberately.*

But still another part of Kipling would suddenly have seen— he might even later have written it down, according to the dictates of his Dæmon—a story about a boy who is abandoned in a little room, grimy, with spiders in every corner, and after a while the spiders come a little nearer, and a little nearer, and one of them is Father Spider, and one of them is Mother Spider, and the boy is their Baby Spider. To Kipling the world was a dark forest full of families: so that when your father and mother leave you in the forest to die, the wolves that come to eat your are always Father Wolf and Mother Wolf, your real father and real mother, and you are—as not even the little wolves ever quite are—their real son. The family romance, the two families of the Hero, have so predominant a place in no other writer. Kipling never said a word or thought a thought against his parents, "both so entirely comprehending that except in trivial matters we had hardly need of words"; few writers have made authority so tender, beautiful, and final—have had us miserable mortals serve better masters; *but* Kipling's Dæmon kept bringing Kipling stories in which wild animals turn out to be the abandoned Mowgli's real father and mother, a heathen Lama turns out to be the orphaned Kim's real father— and Kipling wrote down the stories and read them aloud to his father and mother.

This is all very absurd, all very pathetic? Oh yes, that's very likely; but, reader, down in the darkness where the wishes sleep, snuggled together like bats, you and I are Baby Spider too. If you think *this* absurd you should read Tolstoy—all of Tolstoy. But I should remark, now, on something that any reader of Kipling will notice: that though he can seem extraordinarily penetrating or intelligent—inspired, even—he can also seem very foolish or very blind. This is a characteristic of the immortals from which only we mortals are free. They oversay everything. It is only ordinary readers and writers who have ordinary common sense, who are able to feel about things what

an ordinary sensible man should. To another age, of course,
our ordinary common sense will seem very very common and ordinary, but not sense, exactly: sense never lasts for long; instead
of having created our own personal day-dream or nightmare,
as the immortals do, we merely have consented to the general day-dream or nightmare which our age accepted as reality—
it will seem to posterity only sense to say so, and it will say so,
before settling back into a common sense of its own.

In the relations of mortals and immortals, yesterday's and
today's posterities, there is a certain pathos or absurdity. There
is a certain absurdity in my trying to persuade you to read
Kipling sympathetically—who are *we* to read or not read
Kipling sympathetically? part of me grunts. Writing about just
which writers people are or are not attracted to, these years—
who was high in the 19th, who's low in the 20th—all the other
stock-market quotations of the centuries, makes me feel how
much such things have to do with history, and how little with
literature. The stories themselves are literature. While their
taste is on my tongue, I can't help feeling that virtue is its
own reward, that good writing will take care of itself. It is a
feeling I have often had after reading all of an author: that
there it is. I can see that if I don't write this about the stories,
plenty of other writers will; that if you don't read the stories,
plenty of readers will. The man Kipling, the myth Kipling is
over; but the stories themselves—Kipling—have all the time
in the world. The stories—some of them—can say to us with
the calm of anything that has completely realized its own
nature: "Worry about yourselves, not us. *We're* all right."

And yet, I'd be sorry to have missed them, I'd be sorry for you
to miss them. I have read one more time what I've read so
often before, and have picked for you what seem—to a loving
and inveterate reader, one ashamed of their faults and exalted
by their virtues—fifty of Kipling's best stories.

Steven Marcus

[Stalky & Co.]*

STALKY & CO. is a fantasy and a celebration. It is an idealized recollection and re-creation of Kipling's experience at school. It celebrates a period of life and a way of life, or culture. The period of life is what was once called boyhood. The way of life or culture is that of the English Public School, in this case the United Services College, founded in 1874 by a group of army officers who wanted to provide their sons with an education suited to their class and family, but who could not afford to send them to the more expensive schools. Most of the boys who attended the United Services College were soldiers' sons, and many of them had been born in India. At the College the boys were prepared for the Army Entrance Examination, for most of them were, in their careers, to follow in their fathers' footsteps. By extension, then, *Stalky & Co.* celebrates the way of life of the British Army—of its officer class—and of the Empire which it helped to administer and rule. This Empire and its way of life have ceased significantly to exist (and there is reason to doubt whether they ever existed in the manner that Kipling would have us believe). As a result, *Stalky & Co.* is the celebration of a dead culture, a culture that may seem to many Americans as remote and strange as that of Sparta or the Roman Empire.

Whether the period of life—boyhood—which *Stalky & Co.*

* [From the Introduction to *Stalky & Co.* (New York, 1962). Copyright, 1963 by the Crowell-Collier Publishing Co. Reprinted by permission of the publisher.]

celebrates still exists is perhaps something of an open question. It is certain, however, that our modern conceptions of childhood and adolescence are very different from Kipling's and the nineteenth century's conceptions of boyhood and youth. The very change in the words we use to represent those years of life indicates a change in our idea of them—and a change in ideals and values as well. One of the many uses to which a book like *Stalky & Co.* may be put is that it helps us define and understand ourselves by showing us what, in part, we no longer are. No reader of this book will need to be convinced that in our time the period of adolescence is undergoing a crisis and disturbance of peculiar intensity; or that this crisis is nothing if not one of value and of the authority of value; or that what is being registered so painfully, explosively, and honestly in adolescence is expressive of a general social condition. Among its many other qualities, *Stalky & Co.* will be understood to possess the quality of speaking with intimacy and relevance to this situation.

No doubt this is weighty significance to place upon a book that has for generations been an almost exclusive possession of schoolboys. And there can be little question that its appeal will continue so long as readers enjoy jokes, gags, japes, comic plots and revenges, and the life of free-wheeling fantasy. Yet we should note that if *Stalky & Co.* has been a much loved book, it has also been much hated. The strong word here is accurate, and we should not mistake the matter: it has been hated precisely for its values, or what its values have been taken to be. The school life that it describes is harsh, cruel, and often brutal, and Kipling has been accused of siding with the cruelty and justifying the brutality. The boys are being trained for a life in which force and violence are to be met every day, and Kipling has been charged with affirming the domination of the weak by the strong. The boys are to become part of the governing caste of the British Empire, and Kipling has been accused of uncritically supporting—and as being the propagandist of—the moral values of imperialism and the imperialist system.

These accusations are in one degree or another substantially true. It would be pointless to deny them and almost equally so to try to mitigate them. It might, for example, be argued that although the British Empire was a bad thing, it was still, as George Orwell once remarked, a great deal better than the younger empires that have supplanted it. However true and useful Orwell's remark might be, to introduce it into a discussion of *Stalky & Co.* would act more to distract the reader's attention than to extenuate Kipling. The point to be grasped is that among and alongside all these bad attitudes which seem calculated to outrage the values that most educated persons today affirm—values which can be roughly summed up in the term liberal democracy—there exist other attitudes and values whose absence from contemporary life we all feel and are probably the worse for. These values are described by old, obsolete words like honor, truthfulness, loyalty, manliness, pride, straightforwardness, courage, self-sacrifice, and heroism. That these virtues exist as active and credible possibilities in the world of *Stalky & Co.*, and that they seem not to in ours—or if they do, appear almost solely in corrupted forms—must give us pause. Such a fact may serve to remind us that the moral benefits, conveniences, and superiorities of modern democratic society have not been acquired without cost. Part of this cost seems pretty clearly to have been paid by a diminution of the older masculine virtues. These virtues were felt to exist in the societies of the past, and that they existed in conjunction with the injustices of class, the inequalities of inherited privilege, and with all the offenses against human dignity of which the social past is grossly guilty, should act to increase our awareness of the tragically paradoxical character of social progress. In the moral life of history there are apparently no gains without losses. Few books urge us to confront this contradiction more barely and boldly than *Stalky & Co.*

Yet it would be an oversight to consider *Stalky & Co.* solely from the point of view of social comment and in isolation from its place in literature. It belongs to a genre of literature peculiarly characteristic of the modern era. This literature is concerned with the discovery, examination, and commemoration of childhood and boyhood—especially one's own. It be-

gins with Rousseau's *Émile* and the poetry of Blake and
Wordsworth and is carried forward in the English and American
novel, most notably in Dickens, George Eliot, and Mark Twain.
Although a serious concern with childhood is a common feature
of all modern culture, in no other culture has that concern been
so central and intense as in the culture of the English-speaking
world. In no other language does the word for boy have the
kind of resonance that it does in English. *Garçon, knabe,
muchacho,* are good enough words in their way, but they do
not take away the winter of desolation or make the buds un-
fold or cause one's moral being to rejoice in the way that the
word boy does. In what other language is there such an epithet
as "Oh, boy!"—an expression of the very essence of spontaneous
delight. Or in what other language are lines such as

> Shades of the prison-house begin to close
> Upon the growing boy

thought of as expressing the very essence of sadness, and of
the human condition. In *Stalky & Co.*, when the triumvirate
are publicly rubbing in their revenge on King's house, one of
the masters who is being mercilessly imitated overhears what
is going on and murmurs to another " 'It's not brutality,' . . .
as though answering a question no one had asked. 'It's boy;
only boy.' " Clearly the word is being used here in a metaphysical sense and as descriptive of a metaphysical state. In
short, boy is one of the sacred words of the English language;
boyhood is—or for one hundred and fifty years was—a priestly
state or condition; and the literature of boys and boyhood
has had, for a secularized era, something of the aura of doc-
trinal or holy writ.

One of the chief characters in which the boy appears is as
a schoolboy. English literature is particularly rich in the literature of school (as opposed to America, where the boy tends
more often to be regarded in his relation to nature). This
unique richness is in accord with the unique importance that
education has been given in English tradition and history, and
with the unique English feeling for the experience of education—a feeling which may be summed up in D. W. Brogan's
epigram that England is the only country in the world where

being a schoolboy is an end in itself. This does not mean that going to school is not also a means to an end, or, as we say today, a preparation for life. It does mean, however, that school is first and foremost an experience, like all other experience, and that it is to be thought of, judged, and respected as such. It also means that the best way to ensure the success of educational means is to insist upon them as ends; conversely, the surest way to destroy belief in the value and reality of any effort is to make clear that it is not self-justifying or autonomous. Finally, the statement implies that since being a school boy has such a special weight and significance, much of one's later experience as a man will itself be justified in the degree that it bears out or is in accord with the values of one's earlier experience. As we see in *Stalky & Co.*, the names that the boys give themselves at school are the names by which they greet and recognize each other for the rest of their lives. And for the rest of their lives—no matter what their age—they think of themselves as "Old Boys," not graduates or alumni as we think of ourselves, neutralizing the sex in one case and fleeing from the language in the other. The brute emotion, the unabashed sentimentality of that phrase "Old Boy" is still another indication of the fierce importance with which the English experience of school has traditionally been felt. Such a phrase also reveals the direction in which character will be distorted by an unremitting application of its idea.

Stalky & Co. is a classic of this sub-genre of literature. That it emerges from and refers to a literature which deals with life at school we learn from the book itself, where such popular works as *Eric; or Little by Little* are mentioned only to be held up to comic contempt. These tales, as the reader might suspect, were largely didactic and moralistic in purpose. They dealt with good little boys from home who fell prey to the infinite temptations to immoral behavior at school and who, on the very brink of irredeemable corruption, were saved only by an intervention of moral reform, corporal punishment, or religious conversion. Usually it was a combination of all three. Odd as it may seem today, these books probably served a purpose in their own time. But by and large they served it

badly and falsely, and one of the intentions of *Stalky & Co.* is to alter the picture of life at school presented in these books and to set the record straight.

One of these books, the most famous of them, is significantly not mentioned in *Stalky & Co.* Thomas Hughes's *Tom Brown's Schooldays* is a work of considerable historical importance. The story of a boy's experiences at Rugby during the early years of Thomas Arnold's headmastership, it records with sharp realism the terrible, inhumane life of an English Public School before Arnold's reforms were instituted, and the salutary effect on mind, spirit, and morale that those reforms had when they took hold. It is a work of high Victorian seriousness and moral earnestness, dedicated to the liberal, humane, responsible, and intelligent values which Dr. Arnold's educational ideas and reforms were founded on and which it was his purpose to instill among his students. In its own minor way, *Tom Brown's Schooldays* is a distinguished book, and though it is carefully not mentioned in *Stalky & Co.*, it is always there in the background. Kipling could not in fact have written his work without the precedent of *Tom Brown's Schooldays*; and *Stalky & Co.* may be described as both anti-*Tom Brown* and *Tom Brown* revived. Kipling may have had this in mind when he once referred to *Stalky & Co.* as a moral tract.

All ideals become corrupted in practice, by application to practical life, and the longer any practice persists unchanged, the more corrupt it will grow—this, incidentally, is one of the sounder arguments for the necessity of constant criticism and reform. By the late Victorian period—1875–1900—the high ideals of Arnold and *Tom Brown* had succeeded in penetrating and reforming much of English thinking about school and school life. They had succeeded so well and had been so thoroughly assimilated that they seemed well on the way to turning into their own corrupt opposites. And the forms that cruelty, injustice, pettifogging, and hypocrisy take in *Stalky & Co.* are, by and large, the forms of corrupted Victorian idealism. In such a context, the anti-*Tom Brown*ism of Stalky, M'Turk, and Beetle takes on meaning. The boys' disdain of organized games, their refusal to be moved by petitions in

the name of "the honour of the house," their systematic flout-
ing of appeals to their sense of moral decency and honesty
(as in the "combined" work that goes on in their study),
their contemptuous disregard for the entire prefectorial system, even their inconsistent anti-clericalism, are in considerable
measure a result of their revulsion from what today we would
call the phoniness into which these ideals and values had descended. That the boys are not opposed to these ideals in
themselves, that their rebelliousness is in fact intuitively di-
rected by their feeling for them, is among the major burdens
of the message which *Stalky & Co.* communicates. It is in this
sense that we must think of it as a *Tom Brown* revived.

It should be clear by now that in *Stalky & Co.* we are faced
with a moral situation of some complexity and probably of
deep-seated contradiction. This situation is represented most
forcefully in the variety of attitudes we find both Kipling and
the boys taking toward authority and institutions—that is, institutional authority—and toward the social system which the
institutions serve and whose nature they express. That a writer's
attitude toward social and institutional authority should be
complex, ambivalent, and even contradictory is no more than
what we, in the modern world, have become accustomed
to expect. But to find this attitude in Kipling may be something
of a surprise, since the side of his writing that has drawn the
most conspicuous attention in the last thirty years is the side
that maintained a friendly or affirmative, not to say submis-
sive, attitude toward authority. And if we use the word authority, then we must also use its derived form, authoritarian,
for almost all criticism of Kipling boils down to the accusation
of authoritarianism. That there is an impulse toward it and a
streak of it in him, no open-minded reader will deny; but
that this impulse is checked by other and opposite impulses
which, working together, make for a condition of moral stress
and ambiguity the open-minded reader will also see. Why these
countering impulses should have been overlooked is an historical
question of some complexity. The fact of their having been
overlooked, however, may serve to indicate the distance that
separates our own age and attitudes from Kipling's.

We find these attitudes represented in the boys' relations

with the various masters and with the Head. The modern reader may find the open and mutual antagonism between the boys and masters disturbing because of the book's assumption that this antagonism is natural and proper, and because of the directness, intensity, and ferocity with which the antagonism is enacted on both sides. We don't believe in the propriety or inevitability of such antagonism today; we believe in the cooperative and conciliatory virtues, and distrust the powers of our own aggressiveness so thoroughly that we have almost forgotten how to deal with them—and in the forgetting we have, among other things, palpably increased the likelihood of the world's being blown up. In addition, we are troubled by the kind of freedom that a situation of outright and assumed hostility provides for both sides. All questions of fantasy notwithstanding, the free-wheeling aggressiveness and baiting by both boys and masters in *Stalky & Co.* would today undoubtedly be regarded as pathological conduct. And with a certain justness, for such behavior made sense only within a certain context. This "context" is the Head, and what he stands for. He represents, for both boys and masters, an authority which can be believed in and trusted. He is a court of appeal to which one resorts with faith, and a source of justice whose verdicts one accepts with trust. He represents experience humanized into wisdom, benevolent intelligence, and responsible power. We may think of him as a surrogate for God, as the perfect substitute father for all his orphaned charges, as the idealized voice of society—for he is all these, at least in the eyes of the boys. Whether he or anyone could ever actually embody such qualities and powers is not immediately to the point; what matters is that the boys believe he does, and that, through his conduct toward them, he is able to sustain their belief. Because of this he is able to sustain in them the belief that life itself has certain values, and that one's career in life may have as its legitimate purpose the extension and enlargement of those values.

With this we come to the secret life of *Stalky & Co.*, and to the secret which Kipling, like all distinguished writers about boyhood, has grasped. It is that boys live a life which is passionately moral. Half of the intensity, difficulty, and refractoriness of boys may be traced to the fact that their passionate moral demands on life seem, in the sad course of things, bound to be frustrated and betrayed. As the reader of *Stalky & Co.* will soon discover, boys are by nature moral casuists of genius; they are religious fanatics for justice, and the last true believers in the divinity of law. Boys slavishly worship tradition, blindly reverence ritual, and are the untamed partisans of precedent. They are individually and in aggregate the most naturally conservative, if not reactionary, social grouping—they *want* to believe in the doctrines and ideals that have been officially handed down to them. And we can, without exaggeration, say that every liberal or radical has within him a boy who once found out that "they" were telling him lies, who discovered hypocrisy, sloth, and double-dealing in his elders and superiors. The failure of conservatism has always been a moral failure.

This is not to say that boys devote all their time to inspecting each other's moral fingernails, or that they are not naturally disobedient and do not chafe at discipline and restrictions. That they are and do is written large on every page of *Stalky & Co.* Neither can one say that their ardent moral life can be approached directly and in morality's own terms. When Beetle once complains that King has been unfair, Stalky reproves him: "You've been here six years, and you expect fairness. Well, you *are* a dithering idiot." And after they have exacted retribution on the school bullies, Stalky dryly remarks, "If I knew anything about it, I swear I'd give you a moral lecture." Living in an age and atmosphere in which they have been shot at with moral bullets since infancy, the boys are preternaturally gun-shy of all the cheapened and canting terms of value. (The great creative genius of the Victorian age, Dickens, was almost unable to use the word "moral" in any but an ironic sense—so debased had its currency become.) When the Head chooses to punish the boys, he tells them he is about to perpetrate a howling and flagrant "injustice." Only in this way can he distinguish his moral decisions from those of the lesser masters, which are always of course "just." At a later moment he makes this characteristic distinction in regard to the boys' misbehavior: "I can connive at immorality, but I cannot stand impudence." Given the world of 1880, the Head can make sense only by standing these terms on their heads; and only a man who has the intelligence and courage to do that can reach the moral world in which boys live. Today a gifted teacher of youth would be forced to do something very similar with words like tolerance, cooperation, equality, getting along with the group, and love.

Kipling understood that the moral life of boys is at once extremely primitive and simple, and extremely sophisticated and complex. The virtues to which boys most avidly give themselves are the primitive, ancient, classical, masculine ones —what were known in the past as the heroic virtues. They boys in *Stalky & Co.* are being prepared for an arduous military life, and there is no mistaking the connection between their fantastic exploits at school and their heroic exploits on the Northwest frontier—such is clearly Kipling's intention. But we should realize that there is a heroism in *Stalky & Co.* superior to physical conquest and martial prowess, though it coexists with them. By common consent, the most heroic deed in the book is the Head's saving of a boy's life by sucking the membranous film of diphtheria from his throat. The point of such heroism is in its disregard of self, in its self-sacrifice. And we might recall that the ideal of self-sacrifice is not foreign to the soldierly tradition—at least in its older style. It was this ideal which moved Don Quixote to assert the superiority of the profession of arms to the profession of letters. By means of it we can in part account for the extraordinary affection in which the English still hold Nelson. It was this ideal that Ruskin— the same Ruskin read by M'Turk—had in mind when he declared that the soldier's trade is not slaying, but being slain. In an age like our own in which the military tradition has suffered a degradation which has put it almost beyond redemption, it might be useful to recall that in the past, intelligent men were able to see something noble and humane even in this most destructive mode of human behavior.

Yet these values and ideals, though they are a constant presence in the lives of the boys in *Stalky & Co.*, are never to be discussed, as we learned in the episode, "The Flag of their Country." There the brash, vulgar, and jingoistic Conservative Member of Parliament violates the reserve and offends the soul of every boy in the school by speaking about patriotism and waving the flag in their faces. "In a raucous voice he cried aloud little matters, like the hope of Honour and the dream of Glory, that boys do not discuss even with their most intimate equals; cheerfully assuming that, till he spoke, they had never considered these possibilities." The complexity and sophistication of the moral life which Kipling depicts in *Stalky & Co.* has to do with the fact that the values which inform it are precisely those which are never to be explicitly referred to— like the true name of God, they are too sacred to be spoken— except in parody, joke, or absolute understatement. "Don't you want to die for your giddy country?" M'Turk quizzes Stalky. "Not if I can jolly well avoid it," is the ritual answer.

This quality of indirectness leads us to observe that modern readers will find a certain obscurity and difficulty in reading this book. The obscurity exists in the speech of the boys and is a result of the fact that they speak elliptically and in code. All companies of boys have an argot, a lingo, a code by which they exclude others and help to identify themselves. The code of speech in *Stalky & Co.* is exceptional because of its severity, economy, and power of compression—all of these attributes of Kipling's prose as well. The danger and weakness of any code is that it tends to become excessively limiting, rigid, and self-referring, and to exclude the user from large areas of experience. In *Stalky & Co.*, however, the code in which the boys speak resonates and is confluent with the life for which they are being trained and with its code. What used to be known as the life of an officer and a gentleman was regulated by a strict and complex code. The mastery of this code of living is the object of the education described in this book. By means of it the boys were to learn, supposedly, to rule a vast, primitive colonial Empire, successfully and with relative decency; they were being taught to play what Kipling elsewhere called "the Great Game." The weaknesses of such a conception are manifest: to think of life as a Great Game is to run the risk of never growing up; it is also to run the risk of thinking that there are, in the end, winners and losers in life, a more subtle and profound moral danger. But the strengths of such a conception are too easily by-passed: if life is a Great Game, then there are certain rules of play or conduct which are not to be violated; to violate them is to do worse than lose—it is to put oneself out of consideration altogether. The history of the twentieth century has seen the steady attrition of this ideal; and one of the bitterest accommodations that thoughtful and feeling persons, especially young persons, have had to make is to a world in which this ideal possibility of human conduct is not merely violated and flouted, but made to seem irrelevant, foolish, and naive.

Kipling's consuming interest in a code of life brings us finally to the two modern writers in whom his influence is largest—Ernest Hemingway and Isaac Babel. Both were permanently preoccupied with the heroic code; both took as their central concern the problem of how man is to confront with honor the tragic life of violence that has been his inescapable fate in modern civilization. Like Kipling, both were strongly involved with the life and ideals of boyhood, with conceptions of masculinity and manliness, and with adventure, and the life out-of-doors, these latter our twentieth century equivalents for the nineteenth century's idea of nature. Both were deeply influenced by Kipling's style as well, with its incisive force, speed, and dramatic economy. Hemingway's indebtedness to Kipling is unmistakable and important. Babel's is less well-known but in its way even more interesting.

In his "Reminiscences of Babel," the Russian writer Konstantin Paustovsky tells of their first meeting. It took place in Odessa, shortly after the Revolution. Paustovsky was working in the editorial offices of a magazine called *The Seaman* which had recently published one of Babel's stories. One day Babel was brought to the magazine's offices to meet the editors. He arrived carrying a volume of Kipling under his arm, which he put down on the table but kept looking at it impatiently throughout the polite general conversation. At the first opportunity, Paustovsky remarks, "Babel switched the conversation to Kipling. Writers, he said, should write in Kipling's iron-clad prose; authors should have the clearest possible notion of what was to come out of their pens. A short story must have the precision of a military communiqué or a bank check. It must be written in the same straightforward hand one uses for commands and checks. Kipling's hand was just like that."

He then concluded with this unexpected statement. "Here in Odessa," he said with a note of irony, "we don't produce any Kiplings. We like a peaceful, easy life. But to make up for it, we'll have our home-grown Maupassants." He then left the office. Paustovsky watched him from the window. The moment Babel was out in the street, he "opened his Kipling and started to read as he went. Now and then he stopped to give passers-by a chance to go round him, but he never once raised his head to look at them."

It is, of course, a charming story. Babel's remarks about Kipling are very much to the point, and the discrimination he makes between Kipling and Maupassant, and the choice implied in it, has the same kind of force that, in an earlier generation, Joseph Conrad's decision to write in English rather than French had. But there is something wonderfully ironic and apt about the entire incident. That Kipling, the arch-imperialist and reactionary, should wind up in the hands of a Russian-Jewish revolutionary writer is curious and paradoxical, though not unprecendented: literary influence, fortunately, is not bound in by politics. But that the values of Kipling's prose style—and the moral values which that style embodies and implies—should be precisely the values Babel desired for his own radical and revolutionary writing cannot fail to be a surprise. But, when one thinks about it for a while, there is something very right about it all.

Elliot L. Gilbert

"Without Benefit of Clergy":
A Farewell to Ritual *

> "Now, therefore, give ear to my words,
> and meet your good luck in this way.
> Think which of all your treasures you
> value most and can least bear to part
> with; take it, whatsoever it be, and throw
> it away, so that it may be sure never to
> come any more into the sight of men."
> —Herodotus

I

"Without Benefit of Clergy" has suffered the fate of many
Kipling short stories. Critics have praised it extravagantly as
one of the best of its author's productions—indeed, as one of
the best short stories of all time [1]—and yet have been strangely
reluctant to discuss the work at any length, or to say, after
serious analysis, what it is all about. To be sure, many Kipling
commentators did their work a long time ago when critical
standards were different from what they are today, but even so
recent a writer on the subject as J. M. S. Tompkins has said of
"Without Benefit of Clergy" that it does not require interpretation but "needs only to be displayed." [2] The implication is
that the tale is so transparent and that its meaning is so immediately clear that no analysis of it is necessary. Yet the many
mistaken notions that circulate about the story would seem to
suggest the need for more and not less critical attention.

There are, for example, commentators [3] who wrongly deal

---

* Copyright, 1963 by the author and reprinted with his permission.

1 F. T. Cooper, *Some English Story-Tellers* (New York, 1912), p. 142.
See also W. Somerset Maugham, "Introduction," *Maugham's Choice of
Kipling's Best* (New York, 1953), p. xx.

2 J. M. S. Tompkins, *The Art of Rudyard Kipling* (London, 1959), p.
118.

3 George McMunn, for example, in *Rudyard Kipling: Craftsman* (London, 1937), p. 151 ff.

with the work as a series of tender and touching domestic vignettes. They do this perhaps not so much because they fail to sense the real bitterness and power of the piece as because Kipling wrote so little that might be described in terms of gentleness, and it is always a temptation to create for a favored author a reputation for universality. One critic, in particular, dismisses the tale disparagingly as "one of those super-romantic attachments which now and again some Briton forms" [4]—a gross misreading. Still another, F. T. Cooper, interprets the story as a warning against intermarriage, which it manifestly is not, thus reducing a first-rate work of art to the level of a sociological tract. Cooper even goes so far as to accuse Kipling of having done badly what the author never intended to do at all, writing that

as a protest against racial intermarriage the argument is weakened by the forms of death of the mother and child—because it is impossible to hold the mixed marriage responsible for the fact that an epidemic of fever and of cholera happens to choose this particular woman and child among the victims. [5]

Under these circumstances of confusion and error, a careful reading of the text is necessary. And in fact no Kipling story more richly repays such study. The author was at the height of his considerable narrative and poetic powers when he wrote this work, and he constructed in it a rich and multilayered tale which, in spite of its complexity, moves simply and without a trace of strain through the daily experiences of two lovers to an overwhelmingly tragic vision of life. Kipling's theme is nothing less than the enormous hostility of the universe, the uselessness of man's poor shifts to avoid his fate, and finally, the one painful victory that may sometimes be wrung from life when victory is least expected.

The universe pictured in "Without Benefit of Clergy" is blundering, directionless and very nearly incapable of supporting human life. If it operates at all on any rational principles, these principles are concealed from man, who, in his remote corner of the cosmos, sees only meaningless, random violence

4 Francis Adams, quoted in McMunn, p. 151.
5 F. T. Cooper, p. 128.

and the constant threat of accidental annihilation.[6] Holden's thoughts, in the course of the story, are constantly filled with visions of death; his sensations are at one point described as those of a man who has attended his own funeral.

It is through Holden, through his experiences and his persistent premonitions, that we come to sense the precariousness of life. When Ameera is about to give birth and Holden must leave her for two weeks, he writes out in his own hand a wire announcing her death, leaves it with a servant, and then spends each day grimly awaiting its arrival. Later, when cholera has broken out, the two lovers "kiss each other and shiver," and Holden hesitates about going to his office, thinking that "there were twelve hours in each day when he could not see Ameera, and she might die in three. He was absolutely certain that her death would be demanded." Holden's colleagues collapse overnight and are replaced before they can be missed, only a laconic telegram recording the fact that they ever existed. "Ricketts, Myndonie. Dying. Holden relieve. Immediate."

This threat of disaster broods over the whole story and the sense of the irrationality of life is always lurking in the background. The people of India wait dully for the rains that do not come and that no action of theirs can bring. They watch hopelessly as the drought turns the earth to iron and brings with it the promise of death, a death that is doubly terrible because it is as cheap as life and no more significant. Under the "red and heavy audit" all men are helpless. "The land was very sick and needed a little breathing-space ere the torrent of cheap life could flood it anew. The children of immature fathers and undeveloped mothers made no resistance. They were cowed and sat still, waiting till the sword should be sheathed in November if it were so willed." The end of the terror, it appears, will be no less accidental, no more meaningful, than its beginning.

6 In this connection, F. T. Cooper has written (p. xxx) that Kipling's early stories, such as "Without Benefit of Clergy," involved disinterested fate too much and lacked the sense of inevitability that good stories should have. This is a rather conventional judgment which fails to take into consideration the fact that a random, irrational universe is one of Kipling's most persistent visions. For a fuller discussion of this point see my analysis of "Mrs. Bathurst," *PMLA*, LXXVII, 4 (September, 1962), 450–458.

This grim picture of a universe indifferent or inimical to man turns up regularly in Kipling's fiction, frequently as the main theme. In "Without Benefit of Clergy," however, the emphasis is not so much on the fact of the irrationality of things as it is on people's reactions to that irrationality. Life's essential insanity is taken pretty much for granted by the people who live in the plague-ridden corner of India in which the story is set. These people are resigned to death being sudden and violent and unreasonable. Their resignation, however, does not reduce their need for reassurance and peace; if anything, it intensifies that need and sends them off in search of spiritual comfort. And Kipling follows them in that search, examining the conventions, the ceremonies and the rituals which they have developed to ease the burden of life's uncertainty. It is in this way, incidentally, that intermarriage becomes thematically significant in the story. The meeting of two civilizations in the love of Holden and Ameera gives Kipling the opportunity to describe two sets of rituals as they confront a common disaster, and to consider, especially, their influences on one another.

II

The rituals of the two worlds have more in common than may at first appear. True, the native ceremonies are based largely on superstition while the British customs seem more scientifically or psychologically defensible. The classic English insistence, for example, on "dressing for dinner in the jungle," performs the very real function of maintaining inner discipline and a sense of order. And, of course, sending wives and children up to the cool hills for the Indian hot weather is, medically speaking, a quite sensible thing to do. Yet a reader of "Without Benefit of Clergy" very soon comes to sense that the appeal of such acts as these, and of others like them, is far more ceremonial than rational; that it is not so much the scientific basis of these customs as the almost mystical pleasure and comfort their repetition gives which accounts for their persistence. Ask a British clubman the reason for some long-established prohibition and his response is likely to be not an explanation —which may, in fact, exist—but rather a flat statement of faith:

"It simply is not done." And it is in this crucial way that English and native ceremonies are so similar. They both fulfill a need for reassurance that has been created by the uncertainty and the hostility of the environment; they both make their appeals primarily to that tough central core of fear in every man that will not yield to reason, and which, in India at any rate, has so much to thrive on.

There are many such British customs and rituals described in detail in "Without Benefit of Clergy." Most of them center around The Club, that little bit of home which the English contrive to set up in each of their Indian compounds. In these clubs the rules are quite elaborate and are very strictly enforced, the more so for being, sometimes, ludicrously inappropriate. When Holden returns to his station, for example, after two weeks of duty in the field, the very last thing in the world he wants to do is to visit the club. Having left Ameera two weeks before when she was on the point of giving birth—a precarious business at best in those days and in that place—he now longs to hurry to his house in the city. Yet his very first act, on returning to the compound, is to spend two hours eating dinner at the club. He is miserable, he chafes at the restriction, but apparently it never occurs to him to skip this ritual meal altogether. He knows that so shocking and enormous a breach of protocol would inevitably endanger the secret of his life with Ameera. Indeed, the very secrecy of that life further testifies to the power of convention. The British, who stand ready at any hour to give their lives for the Indian people, nevertheless balk at accepting them as equals, and drive men like Holden into the desperate subterfuges of a double life.

Holden's acceptance of the club, however, is not simply politic. He genuinely needs what that establishment has to offer, as the other men in the station do. He needs the billiard tables and the shop talk. His love for his Indian wife is real, but the call of the old life is equally real. Ameera, with her deep understanding, knows this and always speaks of the time when her husband, and even her son, will return to their own people. Holden, leaving his wife's bedside and tremendously agitated after the first glimpse of his child, knows quite instinctively where to turn for relief. " 'I never felt like this in my life,'

he thought. 'I'll go to the club and pull myself together.' "
That last phrase is an especially apt one. Indeed, the key to all
the English conventions which Kipling enumerates in "Without Benefit of Clergy," and which are so important to an understanding of the story, is self-control, a pulling of oneself
together, that tradition of reticence which, perhaps quite
automatic in Britain, must, in a place like India, be artificially
kept up. For life in India is, to say the least, blatant. People
eke out their precarious existences literally in the streets, and
death usually fails to observe the amenities. Small wonder that
men for whom understatement is a way of life feel uneasy in
such a lurid world and need conventions to help them face it.
In the club, somehow, self-control is easier to achieve. In the
club the most terrible news of life and death may be communicated dispassionately. "It was the Deputy Commissioner of
Kot-Kumharsen, staying at the club for a day, who lightly told
a tale that made Holden's blood run cold as he overheard the
end." Holden, nervous even in the club about his wife and
child, asks anxiously, but even so a little off-handedly, " 'Is it
the old programme then . . . famine, fever, and cholera?' "
To which the Deputy Commissioner replies with the expected
irony, " 'Oh no. Only local scarcity and an unusual prevalence
of seasonal sickness. You'll find it all in the reports if you live
till next year.' "
   Compared to the reticent and quasi-rational conventions of
the British, the native rites seem almost flamboyantly mystical.
"Without Benefit of Clergy" opens on just such a note of
extravagance, with Holden saying " 'But if it be a girl?' " and
Ameera replying " 'Lord of my life, it cannot be. I have prayed
for so many nights, and sent gifts to Sheikh Badl's shrine so
often, that I know God will give us a son—a man-child that
shall grow into a man.' " A few lines later the girl continues in
the same vein. " 'The mullah of the Patten mosque shall cast
his nativity—God send he be born in an auspicious hour!' "
Kipling is here establishing, of course, in the very first lines of
his story, the theme of ritual as a hedge against disaster. But
these lines only begin to introduce the subject. As we read on
we soon see that the story contains many such references. The
drama is played out, for example, against the background of a

teeming Indian city, crowded with millions of the faithful, who live in the shadows of the mosques and minarets and whose only defense against the terrors of the unknown is a naively hopeful mixture of religion and magic. Kipling does not overdo this background material. Instead, he lets us glimpse an occasional sacred procession or hear, as if from far away, a muttered prayer rising from the city. Elsewhere, however, and notably in "The City of Dreadful Night," he describes such scenes in detail, with the heat, the disease, the deaths and, floating over the huddled rooftops, the rousing, mysterious challenge of faith, the *Muezzins'* repeated calls to prayer and the answering professions of belief—"I bear witness that there is no God but God." Indeed, these are the very words Ameera whispers into the ears of her baby when the child has been put into her arms for the first time. Though she is only half-conscious, her first impulse is to place her son under the protection of religion.

Magic plays as large a part as religion in the system of rituals which the Indian natives have developed. When, for example, Holden hurries into the room where his wife and child are lying, he steps on a naked dagger that has been placed on the threshold to avert ill-luck. "It broke at the hilt under his impatient heel. 'God is great!' cooed Ameera in the half-light. 'Thou hast taken his misfortunes on thy head.' " Later, when the baby is older, he becomes the object of all of his mother's superstitious hopes and fears. " 'I know a charm to make him wise as Suleiman and Aflatoun [Solomon and Plato],' " Ameera says one day. "She drew from the embroidered bag a handful of almonds. 'See! I give the parrot one half and Tota the other.' " She gives a piece of almond to the child "who ate it slowly with wondering eyes. 'This I will do each day of seven, and without doubt he who is ours will be a bold speaker and wise.' "

Holden is himself a participant in what is the most fully and brilliantly reported of all the native rituals. Coming from his first sight of the child, he encounters his servant, Pir Khan, who is waiting in the courtyard below with two goats and a sabre. When Holden asks bewilderedly what this paraphernalia is for he is told " 'For the birth sacrifice. What else? Otherwise the child being unguarded from fate may die.' " (Kipling's own birth had been "hastened" by the sacrifice of a goat.) Holden, initiated by Ameera into some of the native customs, had long ago learned, almost as a joke, the fitting words to be said on such an occasion. Now, with an overwhelming sense of life's precariousness and of his new responsibility, he does not dare reject any possible protection. "Hardly knowing what he did, Holden cut twice as he muttered the Mahommedan prayer that runs: 'Almighty! In place of this my son I offer life for life, blood for blood, head for head, bone for bone, hair for hair, skin for skin.' "

Ameera, for her part, has learned many of the English rituals from Holden. After all, no one can say for sure who may have discovered the true charm, the unique combination of words and gestures that will infallibly placate the Powers. Thus when she prays, mere common sense dictates that she pray both to the Prophet and to Beebee Miriam [the Virgin Mary]. And later, when she has come to herself again after the death of her baby, she accepts the wisdom of British reticence in the face of jealous gods, and decides she and Holden " 'must make no protestations of delight, but go softly underneath the stars,' " lest God find them out. " 'It is naught, it is naught,' " she says after every moment of happiness, hoping that all the Powers will hear.

III

The Powers, however, do not hear. Whether because they do not listen or because they do not exist we never learn, but they do not hear. Indeed, what is most striking about this story is that in the world which it pictures, ritual—elaborate and hopeful and time-consuming as it is—is of no use at all. Powerless either to alter the decrees of the universe or to prepare men to accept the consequences of those decrees, it is, from beginning to end, pathetic hocus-pocus and nothing more. Pir Khan, himself devoted to ritual, sums this truth up best when he hurries to Holden with the news that Ameera has been stricken with black cholera. " 'When there is a cry in the night,' " he says, " ' and the spirit flutters into the throat, who has a charm that will restore?' " This is just the point that is made earlier in the story when Ameera prays for " 'a man-child that shall grow into a man.' " She does have a son, of course, but in a striking illustration of the low efficiency of ritual, the boy does not live. For all her prayers, Kipling seems to be saying, Ameera is no better served by the gods than she is by the laws of chance.

In a crisis, every sort of ritual is hollow. Holden feels only frustration at the obligatory dinner given for him at the club, and the news he receives there about the cholera epidemic terrifies him as much as it does precisely because it is offered in such a ritualistically off-hand way. When he is in trouble he turns to the traditional solace of work, but work helps him little. Forced to leave Ameera just when she needs him most, he does his work so badly that the fact is noticed by all his colleagues. And when his son dies, he is not "alive to the kindness of the gods" who present him with an "unusually heavy mail that demanded concentrated attention and hard work." Even that most unfailingly restorative of rituals, eating, is useless in the face of Holden's great sorrow. Ahmed Khan's curried eggs are no more helpful in assuaging grief than the knife on the threshold, the sacrifice of the goats or the seven almonds of wisdom were in preventing it.

The utter failure of ritual is suggested in still other ways. During the drought and famine, for example, "the conches in the Hindu temples screamed and bellowed, for the gods were inattentive in those days." Cholera "struck a pilgrim-gathering of half a million at a sacred shrine. Many died at the feet of their god." And once, in a conversation with Holden, Ameera asks " 'Will my prayers be heard?' " Holden's answer is carelessly conventional. " 'God is very good,' " he says. To which Ameera replies, " 'Of that I am not sure.' "

IV

The failure of ritual, a fact which is central to the meaning of "Without Benefit of Clergy," is inevitable given ritual's function, to achieve order in a chaotic world. Different men, of course, conceive of this function in different ways. On the one hand, comparatively primitive people turn to ritual as a

means of ordering the physical universe. They long to control
the forces of life and in their elaborate ceremonies, they often
seem to be presenting to the universe models of behavior in
the forlorn hope that the universe will comply and shape itself
a little closer to their desires. More sophisticated men, on the
other hand, who have surer if less melodramatic methods of
dealing with nature, nevertheless persist in their own adher-
ence to ritual, not so much because they think it will help them
to organize the universe as because they hope that it will help
them to establish a little order in themselves. In either case,
however, the passion for order is a key to the understanding of
ritual.

In this connection, there is a revealing passage early in
"Without Benefit of Clergy" in which Holden, thinking seriously for the first time of the child that is to come, finds that
he cannot help but feel uneasy. "And there was going to be
added to this kingdom a third person whose arrival Holden felt
inclined to resent. It interfered with his perfect happiness.
It disarranged the orderly peace of the house that was his
own." If Holden's reaction is not all that a storybook father's
should be, it at least has the virtue of being honest and, in
addition, of being thoroughly in character. For Holden, we
must not forget, is a young man who has come out to India to
do something about the sprawling subcontinent, the huge,
confusing country which, with its teeming masses of people
and its violence and disease, is the ultimate metaphor for chaos,
just as the British administrative passion is a striking metaphor
for man's desire to impose order on confusion. Thus, in longing
for order and peace in his own house, Holden is only longing for what all men desire and what they often find it necessary
to invent rituals to achieve.

But order, seen in these terms, seems such a thoroughly
respectable goal. If it is indeed order that is the object of ritual, can this same order also be the reason for ritual's failure?
In "Without Benefit of Clergy," as in many other of his stories,
Kipling seems to be suggesting that this is so. Not that he is
sentimental about confusion and incompetence. That is the
last thing in the world he can be accused of. Order obviously

has its place, as the many successes of the British in India testify. There is nothing in the least edifying, for example, about famine, and so we read with a certain satisfaction that "on the heels of the spring-reapings came a cry for bread, and the Government, which had decreed that no man should die of want, sent wheat."

Such an example of control on the political level is certainly to be applauded, and Kipling, as much as any writer, has been quick to celebrate the man of action, the bridge-builder, the engineer, the administrator. But "Without Benefit of Clergy" is not a story about politics. To be sure, in the concentric worlds which surround the little house in the city, policy is everyone's concern. At the club, for instance, the talk is always "beating up round the ever-fresh subject of each man's work." But such talk remains always in the background; we hear very little of it. What we do hear constantly in this story is the long, sometimes interrupted but always renewed, conversation of Holden and Ameera as the two talk together in their room or on the roof of their house about the inexplicable way of the world and about the inordinate difficulty of coming to terms with it. And it is on this level, this personal level, that ritual fails most conspicuously in the story, because, as Kipling shows us, it is on this level that a passion for order is most fruitless and corrupting.

Why this should be so is not difficult to see. A passionate love of order inevitably implies a certain distaste for the truth about the world as it is actually constituted, implies a great longing to substitute for the disorganized reality of today, the perfectly structured artifice of tomorrow. How else explain the Englishman's willingness to die for the India of his plans and schemes and projects, and yet his refusal to accept the Indians, like Ameera, of the here and now? But the cluttered and untidy reality of the present so easily dismissed by orderly men—what is it, Kipling seems to be asking, but the only reality there is? Love, however much one may anticipate it for the future, can only be experienced in the present (the author tries to show), and life, however much one plans it better for tomorrow, can only be lived today. What's more, a law of compensation seems inevitably to apply to life, decreeing that any provision made for the future must be made at the expense of the present, so that no man may grow rich taking money from one pocket and putting it into another.

Ameera, for one, is quick to recognize the operation of this law. For much of the story she is bitter at the thought of how Englishwomen live longer and retain their youth and beauty longer than Indian women do. Always in her mind is the thought that she will soon be old and ugly and that Holden will leave her for one of the *mem-log*. Indeed, when we first meet her she is extremely self-conscious about her status, and her insistence upon defining herself in terms of the white lady seems to be one of her most important rituals. But when she learns that the white women accomplish their miracle by leaving their husbands for the six months of the hot weather and by turning their children over to nurses, her envy turns to contempt, her ritual longing for status vanishes the way all her other rituals vanish in the course of the story as she comes to understand and to accept reality.

The activities of the *mem-log* astound as much as they disgust her. Why should a woman want to live long and be beautiful, she wonders, except for the love of her husband and children? And if this is so, what madness possesses her to give up both husband and children in order to prolong that life and beauty? What end can she hope to achieve by postponing the experience of love from today until tomorrow, especially in a random and irrational universe in which the chance is always great that there will be no tomorrow? From a purely practical point of view, of course, Ameera's own refusal to withdraw to the hills may seem foolishly willful. But in the sense that it represents her passionate commitment to an idea, to the idea that life—infinitely precious and, from all she has seen of it, infinitely tenuous—is meaningful only when it is being lived, that same refusal is shown to be courageous and honest. Thus Kipling is not writing a story about the destructiveness of intermarriage in a society which frowns on it and enforces secrecy. Ameera does not, as one critic has put it, eat herself up in the process of envying the white woman. Her decision to remain

behind in the plains with Holden is based not on embarass-
ment or fear but on love.

"Without Benefit of Clergy" contains other characters
who, like the *mem-log*, have abandoned the reality of human
love to pursue an ephemeral and empty security. Ameera's
old mother is one, her key to order and control being the
acquisition of money and possessions. Having early been left
penniless, she solved her problem by selling Ameera to Holden
and would, we are told, have sold her "shrieking to the Prince
of Darkness if the price had been sufficient." Her reaction to
her daughter's death is especially in character. The girl has
hardly breathed her last when the old woman is at Holden, tormenting him unmercifully about the few sticks of furniture she
hopes to inherit. "In her anxiety to take stock of the house
fittings," Kipling tells us, "she forgot to mourn."

The English administrators at their clubs also suffer from
a mistrust of life which shows up in an exaggerated concern
for order and propriety. Their reticence and their insularity
are only ritualistic ways of postponing or avoiding human
experience. Involved as they are in their work, they are too
preoccupied with the horrors of tomorrow to react today, too
busy constructing safe imitations of their old life to appreciate,
as Holden does, the reality that is all around them. For as
Holden would be the first to admit, the disruption of his
orderly home is a small price to pay for his son. Such reality,
he has learned, is always to be preferred to artifice, and reassuring Ameera one evening, for the thousandth time, that he will
never abandon her for one of the *mem-log*, he says " 'I have
seen fire balloons by the hundred. I have seen the moon, and—
then I saw no more fire balloons.' "

Ritual, then, implies the sacrifice of what we have for what
we think we would prefer, and it is Kipling's purpose in "Without Benefit of Clegy" to expose the terrible fraud of such sacrifice, to show how, in attempting to comfort and reassure us,
it involves us instead in the insane tautology of giving up the
very life we are trying to achieve. " 'Strike!' " says Pir Khan
to Holden, as the Englishman is about to sacrifice the two
goats. " 'Never life came into the world but life was paid for

it.' " To which Holden replies with the words of the prayer, offering " 'life for life, blood for blood, head for head, bone for bone, hair for hair, skin for skin.' "

But nothing will ever be gained, Kipling assures us, from bargains like this. It is not man's business to haggle with the universe (using his most precious commodity—life—as the medium of exchange) no matter what name he gives that haggling, no matter what ritualistic form it may take. It is man's business, rather, to live as richly as he can, postponing nothing, flinching at nothing, recognizing as inevitable that the more he has the more he will lose, that the greater his joy the greater will be his sorrow; yet sacrificing nothing out of cowardice or in the vain hope that he can find a happiness he will not have to pay for. This is the theme of "Without Benefit of Clergy."

In order to express so far-reaching a theme within the framework of a piece of fiction, Kipling has dramatically arrayed two powerful forces against one another. On one side there is a world full of fear and of rituals to drive out fear; there is India, burdened with death and with terror of the unknown, turning to religion and magic in a desperate attempt to find meaning and order in the universe; there are the English in their compound with their conventions and their forms, anxious to serve but too quick, in the name of self-sacrifice, to postpone living to a more auspicious time. On the other side there is the small house in the midst of the city; there is the poignancy of the feeling Holden and Ameera have for one another; there is the child who incarnates their love; there is Holden with his refreshing desire to move beyond the narrow, official experiences of his peers; and most of all, there is Ameera.

v

Considering that she is the most crucial character in the story, Ameera has been badly misunderstood by critics. Walter M. Hart, for example, writes that

Ameera has something of the beauty, the strangeness, the mystery, the elusiveness of the fairies of the Celtic otherworld, beloved of Arthur's knights, and like the amorous adventures of Guingamor, of Guinemar, or Tyolet in the *lais* of Marie de France, her story is removed from reality and the judgments of reality.[7]

Obviously Hart has permitted himself to be misled by Ameera's exotic background and speech into supposing that she herself is not really human and cannot be judged as if she were. In taking such a position he is, first of all, badly underestimating Kipling as an observer of life. It is one thing to expect Europeans and Americans who have never left home to deal in romantic clichés about "dusky maids." It is quite another to think of Kipling, with his keen eye for the realities of Indian life and his even keener desire to communicate those realities, offering to his readers the stereotype which Hart describes.

But there is refutation even nearer at hand; there is the story itself. No one reading even the bare facts of Ameera's life can speak of her story as being removed from reality. Ameera's experiences are elemental and universal and are presented with an extraordinary faithfulness to everyday detail. Moreover her reactions to these experiences are absolutely honest; there is not a trace of the sentimentalist in her. It would be a great mistake, for example, to think that because she addresses her husband in certain conventionally exaggerated terms of self-abasement, her relationship to him is in any sense that of a slave to a master.

On the contrary, the marriage of Ameera and Holden is a genuine marriage precisely because it is founded on mutual

7 Walter M. Hart, *Kipling the Story-Writer* (Berkeley, 1918), p. 70. Hart's conclusion about the story may well have been influenced by the style of the conversations between Holden and Ameera. In Edmund Wilson's words (*The Wound and the Bow*, p. 117) Kipling has his characters "talk an English which translates their own idiom," and it is this speech—full of "thee" and "thou," "my King" and "my Queen"—which has no doubt misled certain critics into reading the story as a quaint, rather sentimental love idyll. This technique, not the same at all as dialect, of course, does, on occasion, help the author to create a heightened and poetic effect, but not one of unreality. With an almost imperceptible adjustment of vision, the reader can see these lines not as passages of stilted, sentimental prose, but as translations into English of expressions which, in the original, are completely idiomatic and unselfconscious. Indeed, Kipling several times tries to help his readers make this adjustment, often by quite plainly calling their attention to the fact that he is translating. At one point, he explains a line which in English seems to have little meaning by indicating that the passage involves a pun in the original.

respect and on honesty, with Ameera, if a choice must be made, even more realistic than her husband. Holden is occasionally guilty of trying to humor his wife, of turning her questions aside, as we have seen, with conventional answers. But Ameera never permits such tactics and never practices them herself. She is no Madame Butterfly, building her life on self-deception. When Holden tries to pretend that the money he paid her mother was a dowry, Ameera instantly replies, " 'What talk is yours of dower! I was bought as though I had been a Lucknow dancing-girl instead of a child.' " And when Holden goes on to ask " 'Art thou sorry for the sale?' " Ameera does not immediately give the easy answer. " 'I have sorrowed,' " she says. Considering all this, it is hard to accept the statement made by J. M. S. Tompkins that Ameera is "entirely ignorant," and that she "is executed by the gods in her ignorance." [8] Ameera is, in fact, the wisest person in "Without Benefit of Clergy," and on her deathbed especially she achieves an insight into reality which cannot be founded on ignorance.

Naturally she was not born wise. At the age of sixteen she brought to a very precipitous marriage all those strange notions, old wives' tales, magical charms and tag ends of dubious advice that a person must make do with in the world before he has acquired some experience of his own. In her addiction to rituals and conventions she is no different from anyone else in the story. Even Holden, with his ability to break away from the rigid formulae of British caste and his painful insight into the precariousness of the world, seems sometimes to have an almost mystical faith in the ability of his wooden gate, guarded by Pir Khan, to keep out the sorrow and danger of life. Sorrow comes to all men, of course, but has the effect of confirming most of them in the wisdom of their retreat behind the wooden gates of ritual and ceremony. What is so remarkable about Ameera is that each blow that life inflicts on her makes her not more and more a prisoner of the superstitions she started with, but somehow more and more free of them. With the death of the little boy, for example, the magic charms vanish from the story and do not return. In their

8 Tompkins, p. 101.

place there appears temporarily that special kind of wariness
of life which Solon counsels in Herodotus and which, at one
time or another, most people have found themselves indulging
in. " 'It was because we loved Tota that he died. The jealousy
of God was upon us,' " Ameera says. " 'We must make no
protestation of delight, but go softly underneath the stars,
lest God find us out.' "

But such a ritual does not satisfy her for long, either. It is
absurdly self-defeating, requiring that she live less in order to
live more, deny love in order to preserve it. As she recovers
slowly from the agony of Tota's death, she senses that a pro-
founder love has grown up between Holden and herself, and
she now comes to understand at least one meaning of her experience. Sorrow, she now feels, is not the ultimate disaster of
life, to be avoided at all costs, even at the expense of life itself,
but rather the inevitable companion of joy beyond which it is
sometimes possible to pass to a joy even more intense. The moment she recognizes this fact, she is free of the enervating drag
of ritual with its useless self-sacrifice, free for the first time to
live without fear.

The last months of her life are the best. "There are not many
happinesses," Kipling writes, summing up the theme of his
story, "so complete as those that are snatched under the shadow
of the sword." Life is all that there is now. "They sat together
and laughed, calling each other openly by every pet name that
could move the wrath of the gods." When death comes at last,
it is merely another random accident, without moral significance.
Holden might just as easily have died in Ameera's place, or they
both might just as easily have survived. Ameera is in a coma
when Holden reaches her bedside. But as the first drops of rain
begin to fall on the roof and as shouts of joy rise from the
parched city at the return of life, she rallies one last time and
expresses her final insight. Holden stoops lower and Ameera
forms her last words on his ear, just as a few years earlier she
had formed on her baby's ear the words of the profession of
faith—"I bear witness that there is no God but God." Only now
the words have been slightly but significantly changed to a profession of a new faith. " 'I bear witness,' " she says, " 'I bear
witness—that there is no God but—thee, beloved!' "

Coming from a woman as honest and as proud as Ameera, this statement is clearly no sentimental hyperbole. Rather, it represents a courageous decision on the girl's part, at the bitter moment of her death, to abandon the comfort of the old religion and to substitute for the ritual of her fathers an affirmation of the truth she has learned in her own life. For the love she has had, Ameera knows and Kipling has skillfully shown us, is the one reality in the world. Everything else is ranged, as Miss Tompkins has suggested, in concentric tiers around that love and grows more and more illusory the further it moves from the warmth at the center. In the first circle lies the world of Holden's job, the paper work and the conventional social relationships. Beyond that, and still dimmer, is England, barely an influence, knowing nothing, understanding nothing, represented by the ridiculous figure of the Member for Lower Tooting who is so ignorant that he singles out for his special approval the very flowers which foretell the disaster that is to come.[9] And beyond everything there is the universe, which, though it may randomly impose suffering and death and turn life to ashes in the mouth, is nevertheless most unreal of all. The only reality is the reality of human love. This is the fact which Ameera affirms with her last breath. Life is lived best when it is lived without fear, without hesitation, without despairing surrender to ritual—in short when it is lived without benefit of clergy.

Kipling's titles are often ambiguous, providing clues to the meanings of his stories which must be searched for diligently. This is especially the case here. Most critics have sensed some of the richness and complexity of this title,[10] have seen that on its most obvious level, it refers to the fact that Holden and Ameera were never properly married. In that sense, the phrase has a

9 His intrusion thus being not "beyond defence," as Miss Tompkins writes, p. 248.

10 See especially Miss Tompkins' analysis, p. 101, and Hart's comments, p. 69. Benefit of clergy, so-called, was a reprieve given by English law to educated and therefore socially valuable criminals, e.g., Ben Jonson, who could prove their literacy by reading a selected passage—the "neck verse." Miss Tompkins points out that Ameera is executed "in her ignorance" because she is unable, figuratively speaking, to read her "neck-verse." I am inclined to think, rather, that in this universe of Kipling's there *are* no "clergy": no one, British or Indian, gets a second chance.

smug and priggish quality, a tone of outraged morality [11] which makes it especially ironic in the face of the exemplary marriage. That, of course, is just the point. It is the uselessness of ceremony, the theme so often reiterated in this story, which gives fullest meaning to the title. "By every rule and law," we are told, the love of Ameera and Holden should not have been possible. But rules and laws are weak things. "It was a contract," we read, "entered into with a light heart," but despite the absence of official sanction it became the most binding contract either of the lovers had ever known. In the last analysis the title represents Kipling's approval of the couple, of their life together, and, particularly, of Ameera's courageous death.

For if it is difficult enough to live without benefit of clergy, it is infinitely harder to die without it, to reject the reassurance that ritual can give and which man so poignantly yearns for at the moment of death. We should not underestimate the magnitude of Ameera's achievement. She dies a bitter death, knowing, and not trying to conceal from herself the knowledge, that her celebration of life, triumphant as it is, inevitably involves recognition of the appalling nothingness that is left when life is gone. "There is *no* God but thee, beloved." Indeed, it is on this very note of utter annihilation that Kipling chooses to end his story, anxious that no reader should finish the work imagining that its final position is one of easy affirmation. Holden rushes away from his dead wife into a torrent of rain. Three days later the downpour has almost obliterated the house and the landlord announces that he will finish the job the rains have begun.

'I will have it pulled down—the timber will sell for something always. It shall be pulled down, and the Municipality shall make a road across, as they desire, from the burning-ghat to the city wall, so that no man may say where this house stood.'

A few days more pass and all traces of the life that had been so ful and had achieved so overwhelming a victory are gone forever.

11 There is a suggestion of this tone in the remark by Cyril Falls that Kipling wove his story "out of material sordid enough." *Rudyard Kipling* (New York, 1915), p. 95.

VI

The tragedy of "Without Benefit of Clergy" is an existential-ist one. In this respect, Kipling foreshadowed many twentieth-century works of fiction not only thematically but in terms of plot structure as well. For example, when Holden hurries away through the rain at the end of the story, leaving his dead wife behind, he does not know that forty years later an even more famous fictional hero will reenact this same scene. Lieutenant Henry and Catherine, the central characters in Hemingway's *A Farewell to Arms*, are in many ways the doubles of Holden and Ameera. Hemingway often acknowledged his literary in-debtedness to Kipling and while it is impossible to establish with any certainty that the earlier story influenced the later, the parallels remain striking. Both couples find love outside the arbitrary bounds which society has established for it, and both nurture that love in a precarious world which threatens them at every moment with separation and death. Both find an almost idyllic happiness in the midst of a holocaust, both are tanta-lized for a brief moment with the hope, which they never quite permit themselves to believe in, of a normal life, and in both cases the women die at a moment of great joy, leaving the men to face emptiness alone.

In theme as well as in plot structure the stories are remark-ably alike. Both Kipling and Hemingway, for example, draw the same conclusions in their stories about the nature of life, con-clusions which by now have become almost the philosophical commonplaces of our generation and which are admirably epitomized in Albert Camus' existentialist vision of an absurd universe. In that universe, in which there are only two basic truths—man's desire for order and his absolute knowledge that he can never achieve it—the human being must learn to live with the absurdity of this enormous contradiction without, on the one hand, accepting the easy answers he finds all about him, or, on the other, abandoning the search for meaning even when confronted with the certainty of failure in that search.

This position is, of course, the one that is taken in both "Without Benefit of Clergy" and in *A Farewell to Arms*; taken with perhaps fewer overtones of self-pity in Kipling's story than in Hemingway's. For Ameera's vision at the end of her life is Camus'. Having known a time when the reassurance of ritual had attracted her, she now sees the price that must be paid for such easy solace. With real strength of will she rejects that comfort, and in the face of her knowledge of the universe's infinite emptiness, affirms the absolute validity of experience.

It is this image of Ameera more than any other single fact about the story which calls into question the traditional critical approaches to "Without Benefit of Clergy." The common error of all the critics has been to think of the story as one which turns its face toward the past; one which attempts, in terms of a sentimental love affair, to reestablish the other-worldly innocence of bygone days. What careful reading of the text shows, however, is that the tale turns not toward the romantic past but to the grimly realistic present, and that it confronts movingly, but with honesty and vigor, life's absurd paradox. The Kipling who emerges from "Without Benefit of Clergy" differs markedly from the Kipling of superficial criticism or popular fancy, and it is time for this different Kipling to be heard.